HAMLYN NEW ALL COLOUR
VEGETARIAN
COOKBOOK

HAMLYN NEW ALL COLOUR
VEGETARIAN
COOKBOOK

HAMLYN

Front cover shows, left to right: Potato jackets with soured cream dip (recipe 169), Vegetarian salad with tarragon mayonnaise (recipe 29), Spinach pancakes (recipe 53).

Back cover shows, clockwise from top left: Button mushrooms with green peppercorns (recipe 93), Rice-stuffed peppers (recipe 153), Chicory, orange and watercress salad (recipe 117), Frozen butterscotch mousse (recipe 193), Gardeners' broth (recipe 1), Malted wholemeal bread (recipe 221).

First published in Great Britain 1993
by Hamlyn, an imprint of Reed Consumer Books Limited
Michelin House, 81 Fulham Road, London SW3 6RB
and Auckland, Melbourne, Singapore and Toronto.

Copyright © 1993 Reed International Books Limited

Line drawings by Coral Mula
Photographs from Reed Consumer Books Picture Library

ISBN 0 600 57834 8

A CIP catalogue record for this book is available from the British Library

Produced by Mandarin Offset
Printed and bound in Hong Kong

OTHER TITLES IN THIS SERIES INCLUDE

Hamlyn All Colour Entertaining
Hamlyn New All Colour Cookbook
Hamlyn All Colour Vegetarian Cookbook
Hamlyn All Colour Indian Cookbook
Hamlyn All Colour Chinese Cookbook
Hamlyn All Colour Salads
Hamlyn All Colour Slimming Cookbook
Hamlyn All Colour Italian Cookbook

CONTENTS

USEFUL FACTS AND FIGURES

NOTES ON METRICATION

In this book quantities are given in metric and Imperial measures. Exact conversion from Imperial to metric measures does not usually give very convenient working quantities and so the metric measures have been rounded off into units of 25 grams. The table below shows the recommended equivalents.

Ounces	Approx g to nearest whole figure	Recommended conversion to nearest unit of 25	Ounces	Approx g to nearest whole figure	Recommended conversion to nearest unit of 25
1	28	25	9	255	250
2	57	50	10	283	275
3	85	75	11	312	300
4	113	100	12	340	350
5	142	150	13	368	375
6	170	175	14	396	400
7	198	200	15	425	425
8	227	225	16(1lb)	454	450

Note

When converting quantities over 16 oz first add the appropriate figures in the centre column, then adjust to the nearest unit of 25. As a general guide, 1kg (1000 g) equals 2.2 lb or about 2 lb 3 oz. This method of conversion gives good results in nearly all cases, although in certain pastry and cake recipes a more accurate conversion is necessary to produce a balanced recipe.

Liquid measures

The millilitre has been used in this book and the following table gives a few examples.

Imperial	Approx ml to nearest whole figure	Recommended ml	Imperial	Approx ml to nearest whole figure	Recommended ml
1/4	142	150 ml	1 pint	567	600 ml
1/2	283	300 ml	1 1/2 pints	851	900 ml
3/4	425	450 ml	1 3/4 pints	992	1000 ml (1 litre)

Spoon measures

All spoon measures given in this book are level unless otherwise stated.

Can sizes

At present, cans are marked with the exact (usually to the nearest whole number) metric equivalent of the Imperial weight of the contents, so we have followed this practice when giving can sizes.

Oven temperatures

The table below gives recommended equivalents.

	°C	°F	Gas Mark		°C	°F	Gas Mark
Very cool	110	225	1/4	Moderately hot	190	375	5
	120	250	1/2		200	400	6
Cool	140	275	1	Hot	220	425	7
	150	300	2		230	450	8
Moderate	160	325	3	Very hot	240	475	9
	180	350	4				

NOTES FOR AMERICAN AND AUSTRALIAN USERS

In America the 8-fl oz measuring cup is used. In Australia metric measures are now used in conjunction with the standard 250-ml measuring cup. The Imperial pint, used in Britain and Australia, is 20 fl oz, while the American pint is 16 fl oz. It is important to remember that the Australian tablespoon differs from both the British and American tablespoons; the table below gives a comparison. The British standard tablespoon, which has been used throughout this book, holds 17.7 ml, the American 14.2 ml, and the Australian 20 ml. A teaspoon holds approximately 5 ml in all three countries.

British	American	Australian
1 teaspoon	1 teaspoon	1 teaspoon
1 tablespoon	1 tablespoon	1 tablespoon
2 tablespoons	3 tablespoons	2 tablespoons
3 1/2 tablespoons	4 tablespoons	3 tablespoons
4 tablespoons	5 tablespoons	3 1/2 tablespoons

AN IMPERIAL/AMERICAN GUIDE TO SOLID AND LIQUID MEASURES

Imperial	American	Imperial	American
Solid measures		Liquid measures	
1 lb butter or		1/4 pint liquid	2/3 cup liquid
margarine	2 cups	1/2 pint	1 1/4 cups
1lb flour	4 cups	3/4 pint	2 cups
1 lb granulated or		1 pint	2 1/2 cups
caster sugar	2 cups	1 1/2 pints	3 3/4 cups
1lb icing sugar	3 cups	2 pints	5 cups
8 oz rice	1 cup		(2 1/2 pints)

NOTE: WHEN MAKING ANY OF THE RECIPES IN THIS BOOK, ONLY FOLLOW ONE SET OF MEASURES AS THEY ARE NOT INTERCHANGEABLE.

INTRODUCTION

The HAMLYN NEW ALL COLOUR VEGETARIAN COOKBOOK is a lively collection of interesting, easy-to-prepare dishes to suit both the beginner and the more experienced cook. With 240 recipes, plus variations, the book offers plenty of choice for all tastes.

Chapters are arranged so that meal planning is easy. Soups and starters open the book, followed by chapters on beans, pulses and grains and main course dishes. Choose a vegetable accompaniment or salad from the following two chapters. If it is a simple supper or snack you are after, choose from the rice and pasta chapter or the selection of light meal recipes. Round off with a dessert or a cake from the baking chapter.

There is a colour photograph for each recipe (including the recipes which open each chapter and which are illustrated on the book's cover), making it easy to see at a glance how the finished dish will look. Preparation and cooking times make meal planning simple, and calorie counts let the weight-conscious decide on the best recipes for them. Those recipes suitable for vegans are labelled, and there are Cook's Tips to give valuable extra information about nutrition, unusual ingredients, techniques, garnishes and sauces.

The wide range of ingredients used in the recipes ensure that the vegetarian cook does not have to rely on a narrow group of foods and flavourings and that the food is interesting as well as nutritionally sound. Grains, beans, pulses and pasta are cooked with fresh vegetables to make delicious combinations. Unusual vegetarian ingredients like tofu add new textures and flavours.

Vegetarians know that dishes containing nuts, pasta, grains and pulses are good sources of protein, as are those with eggs and cheese. Cooks should be careful, though, not to use too many high-fat cheeses such as Cheddar, Stilton or cream cheese. Look for lower fat alternatives like cottage cheese or curd cheese. Eggs should be limited to not more than three a week.

Many cheeses contain animal rennet, a by-product of the meat industry, and vegetarians should look out for those labelled 'suitable for vegetarians'. There is now quite a wide selection of such cheeses available in supermarkets, especially Cheddar, Stilton and cottage cheese. Mozzarella is vegetarian, but it is almost impossible to find a suitable Parmesan, though Italian Pecorino makes an acceptable substitute.

Butter is suitable for vegetarians, but it is also high in saturated fat, so try replacing it with healthier sunflower margarine instead. Use oils high in polyunsaturated fat for cooking, or olive oil, which is high in monounsaturates, for salads and other cooking.

While vegetarians eat eggs, they generally avoid barn or farm fresh eggs, which may be battery in origin. Vegans, of course, do not eats eggs or any dairy products. Gelatine, another by-product of the meat industry, is also not eaten by vegetarians or vegans, and recipes in this book use agar-agar, a suitable vegetable alternative.

All the recipes in the HAMLYN NEW ALL COLOUR VEGETARIAN COOKBOOK make the most of a wide variety of vegetarian ingredients, fresh vegetables and fruit. Using them, you will be able to enjoy a delicious collection of nutritious and healthy treats, whether you are a vegetarian or a vegan, or a healthy eater who simply wants to cut down on meat.

SOUPS & STARTERS

Choose a protein-packed soup containing pulses or nuts for a healthy snack or Light vegetable soup or Carrot and coriander for a first course. A starter or appetiser should create anticipation of what's to follow. Choose dips for a buffet meal, or a lighter starter if a more filling meal of several courses is to follow.

1 GARDENERS' BROTH

Preparation time:
30 minutes

Cooking time:
1¼ hours

Serves 4

Calories:
153 per portion

YOU WILL NEED:
25 g/1 oz butter or soya margarine
2-3 small onions, sliced
2-3 small carrots, sliced
a small piece of turnip, chopped
1 litre/1 ¾ pints vegetable stock or water (see recipe 3)
2 tomatoes, skinned and sliced (see Cook's Tip)
2-3 runner beans, topped and tailed
a few leaves young cabbage, shredded
salt and pepper
pinch of mixed herbs
25 g/1 oz short-cut macaroni
grated vegetarian Cheddar cheese, to sprinkle
1 tablespoon finely chopped fresh parsley

Melt the butter in a large pan and sauté the onions until softened. Add the carrots and turnip and cook for a further 5 minutes. Pour in the stock or water and bring to the boil.

Add the rest of the vegetables, salt and pepper to taste, and herbs, then cover and simmer for 45 minutes. Add the macaroni and simmer for a further 15 minutes.

Serve piping hot sprinkled with grated cheese and chopped parsley.

2 PEA SOUP

Preparation time:
10 minutes plus soaking

Cooking time:
2½-3½ hours

Serves 4-6

Calories:
198-132 per portion

Suitable for vegans

YOU WILL NEED:
1 tablespoon oil
1 onion, chopped
1 garlic clove, crushed
2 celery sticks, chopped
225 g/8 oz dried marrowfat peas, soaked overnight
1.5 litres/2 ½ pints water
1 bouquet garni
salt and pepper
mint sprigs, to garnish

Heat the oil in a large pan, add the onion and cook until softened. Add the garlic and celery and cook for 5 minutes, stirring occasionally.

Drain the peas and add to the pan with the water, bouquet garni and salt and pepper to taste. Cover and boil rapidly for 10 minutes, then simmer gently for 2-3 hours, until the peas are soft. Remove the bouquet garni.

Cool slightly, then place half the soup in an electric blender or food processor and work to a smooth purée. Repeat with the remaining soup. Return to the pan. Reheat the soup gently, adding a little more water if it is too thick. Pour into a warmed tureen and garnish.

■ COOK'S TIP

To skin tomatoes, place them in a bowl and pour over freshly boiling water. Leave for 30-60 seconds, depending on ripeness, then drain and slit the skins which should *slide off easily. Alternatively, hold a tomato on a fork over a gas flame until the skin splits. Turn the tomato slowly all the time.*

■ COOK'S TIP

Swirl a little soured cream, natural yogurt, crème fraîche or plain fromage frais into this soup before serving – delicious!

3   CHINESE LEAF & PEPPER SOUP

Preparation time:
25 minutes

Cooking time:
45 minutes

Serves 4

Calories:
339 per portion

YOU WILL NEED:
2 tablespoons vegetable oil
50 g/2 oz butter
225 g/8 oz green peppers, cored, seeded
  and diced
2 onions, chopped
½ head Chinese leaves, shredded
40 g/1 ½ oz plain flour
450 ml/ ¾ pint vegetable stock (see
  Cook's Tip)
salt and pepper
450 ml/ ¾ pint milk
3 tablespoons single cream

Heat the oil in a saucepan, then add the butter. When melted, add the peppers, onions and Chinese leaves and cook gently for 5 minutes.

Blend in the flour and cook for 1 minute. Gradually stir in the vegetable stock and bring to the boil. Add salt and pepper to taste and simmer, covered, for 30 minutes or until the vegetables are tender.

Purée the soup in a blender or food processor or work through a sieve. Return to the pan, stir in the milk and heat through. Taste and adjust seasoning and just before serving, swirl in the cream.

4   MUSHROOM AND WALNUT SOUP

Preparation time:
10 minutes

Cooking time:
25 minutes

Serves 4

Calories:
188 per portion

YOU WILL NEED:
25 g/1 oz walnut pieces
25 g/1 oz butter
1 medium onion, chopped
100 g/4 oz button mushrooms, roughly
  chopped
900 ml/1 ½ pints vegetable stock (see
  recipe 3)
large pinch of grated nutmeg
salt and pepper
6 tablespoons double cream
FOR THE GARNISH
chopped fresh chives (see Cook's Tip)
chopped walnuts

Cover the walnuts with boiling water and leave for 1 minute. Drain on paper towels.

Melt the butter in a medium pan, add the onion and fry until softened. Add the mushrooms and cook for 1 minute. Stir in the stock, nutmeg, salt and pepper and bring to the boil. Cover and simmer for 15 minutes.

Chop the walnuts in a blender or food processor. Add the cooked vegetables and liquid and blend until the mushrooms are finely chopped. Adjust the seasoning. Chill well.

To serve, stir the cream into the soup and sprinkle with the chives and walnuts.

■ COOK'S TIP

For basic vegetable stock: fry 2 each onions, potatoes, celery sticks (all chopped). Stir in 1 each parsnip, turnip (both sliced). Add 1.2 litres/ 2 pints water and selection of herbs. Simmer 1 hour. Strain and cool.

■ COOK'S TIP

To chop fresh chives, hold the washed bunch firmly and use a pair of scissors to snip them into a small basin. Instead of cream, stir in some Greek yogurt.

5   SPINACH SOUP

Preparation time:
20 minutes

Cooking time:
20 minutes

Serves 4

Calories:
272 per portion

YOU WILL NEED:
*750 g/1 ½ lb fresh spinach, washed
    thoroughly and stalks removed*
25 g/1 oz butter
1 small onion, finely chopped
25 g/1 oz plain flour
*600 ml/1 pint vegetable stock (see
    recipe 3)*
about 300 ml/½ pint milk
salt and pepper
freshly grated nutmeg
FOR THE GARNISH
about 2 tablespoons natural yogurt
4 lemon slices (optional)

Cook the spinach without water in a covered pan for 6-8 minutes, then turn into a bowl. (Heat frozen spinach until just thawed, see Cook's Tip).

Rinse out the pan and melt the butter in it. Add the chopped onion, fry gently without browning for 5 minutes then add the flour. Cook for 3 minutes, then pour in the stock. Stir well, bring to the boil and simmer for 3-4 minutes.

Cool slightly, then pour into a liquidizer or food processor, add the cooked spinach and blend until smooth. Pour back into the pan and stir in sufficient milk to give a pouring consistency. Add salt, pepper and nutmeg to taste. Reheat the soup gently and serve, garnishing each bowl with a swirl of yogurt and a slice of lemon, if liked.

The soup can be frozen for up to 6 weeks. Thaw overnight at room temperature and reheat gently.

▦ COOK'S TIP

If fresh spinach is not available use a 275 g/10 oz pack of frozen spinach instead. Spinach should be cooked for the shortest possible time to retain its *colour and nutritional value, so for this soup it is cooked separately. No water is necessary, as spinach contains a high proportion of water.*

6   LIGHT VEGETABLE SOUP

Preparation time:
30 minutes

Cooking time:
30 minutes

Serves 4

Calories:
114 per portion

YOU WILL NEED:
1 knob butter
1 small onion, finely chopped
*175 g/6 oz carrots, scrubbed and cut
    into narrow matchstick strips*
3 sticks celery, trimmed and sliced
1 teaspoon cornflour
*900 ml/1 ½ pints vegetable stock (see
    recipe 3)*
1 teaspoon tomato purée
2 tablespoons chopped fresh parsley
celery leaves
FOR THE OMELETTE GARNISH
2 eggs
salt and pepper
15 g/½ oz butter

Melt the butter in a large pan and fry the onion gently without browning for about 5 minutes. Add the carrots and celery, cover the pan and cook gently for a few minutes until the butter is absorbed. Stir in the cornflour, then add the stock and tomato purée. Bring to the boil, half cover the pan and simmer for about 20 minutes until the vegetables are tender.

Meanwhile, make the omelette. Beat the eggs with the salt and pepper. Melt the butter in a small frying pan, add the eggs and fry until set and pale brown on the underside. Turn and brown the other side. Cut into 1 cm/½ inch dice.

Taste the soup and season with pepper and a little salt if needed. Stir in the chopped parsley. Serve in bowls garnished with a few pieces of the omelette and a celery leaf.

▦ COOK'S TIP

This vegetable soup can be frozen in a plastic container for up to six weeks, but only make the omelette garnish just before serving.

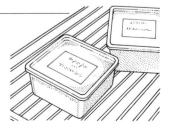

7 ARTICHOKE SOUP

Preparation time:
15 minutes

Cooking time:
30 minutes

Serves 4

Calories:
293 per portion

YOU WILL NEED:
25 g/1 oz butter
1 small onion, thinly sliced
450 g/1 lb Jerusalem artichokes,
* scrubbed and sliced*
salt and pepper
600 ml/1 pint milk
300 ml/ ½ pint vegetable stock (see
* recipe 3)*
chopped fresh chives, to garnish
* (optional)*

Melt the butter in a large pan and fry the onion gently without browning for about 5 minutes. Add the artichokes, cover and cook for a further 5 minutes so that the artichokes completely absorb the butter.

Add salt and pepper then pour in the milk and stock. Bring to the boil and simmer gently, half covered, for about 20 minutes until the artichokes are tender.

Blend in a liquidizer or food processor until smooth. Return the soup to the pan and reheat gently. Taste and adjust the seasoning.

Serve piping hot sprinkled with chives (if liked) and sesame croûtons (see Cook's Tip).

8 VEGETABLE SOUP WITH NORI

Preparation time:
20 minutes

Cooking time:
25 minutes

Serves 4

Calories:
107 per portion

Suitable for vegans

YOU WILL NEED:
2 tablespoons olive oil
2 onions, chopped
4 celery sticks, diced
225 g/8 oz carrots, scraped and diced
350 g/12 oz courgettes, trimmed and
* diced*
225 g/8 oz Chinese leaves or cabbage,
* shredded*
4 garlic cloves, crushed
900 ml/1 ½ pints vegetable stock (see
* recipe 3)*
salt and pepper
2-4 sheets of nori (see Cook's Tip)

Heat the olive oil in a large saucepan and add the onions, celery and carrots. Fry gently for 5 minutes, without letting the vegetables brown, then add the courgettes, cabbage and garlic. Stir and fry gently for a further 5 minutes. Add the stock, bring to the boil, then let the soup simmer for about 15 minutes, until the vegetables are just tender. You can serve the soup as it is, but you may liquidize two cupfuls, then stir this back into the soup. This has the effect of slightly thickening the soup. Season to taste. Serve the soup in bowls and sprinkle with the nori, or serve the nori separately in a small bowl for people to sprinkle over their soup if they like.

■ COOK'S TIP

For the sesame croûtons, cut the crusts from 4 slices of brown bread. Dip each slice into seasoned beaten egg then into sesame seeds. Cut the dipped slices into squares, then cut each square into 2 triangles. Fry in shallow hot oil for about 30 seconds then drain on absorbent kitchen paper.

■ COOK'S TIP

Nori is a seaweed usually sold in dried form. Simply take 2-4 sheets, crisp over a gas flame or under the grill for several seconds, then crumble over the soup.

9 LEEK AND POTATO SOUP

Preparation time:
15 minutes

Cooking time:
25-30 minutes

Serves 6

Calories
155 per portion

YOU WILL NEED:

25 g/1 oz butter or margarine

350 g/12 oz trimmed leeks, washed and
   sliced (see recipe 11)

750 g 1 ½ lb potatoes, peeled and diced

salt and pepper

900 ml/1 ½ pints vegetable stock (see
   recipe 3)

Melt the butter or margarine in a large saucepan, then add the leeks and potatoes and fry these gently with a lid on the pan, for 10 minutes, stirring often. Sprinkle a little salt and pepper over the potatoes and leeks, stir, then continue to cook gently, still covered, for a further 10 minutes, stirring often. It doesn't matter if the vegetables brown slightly, but don't let them get too brown.

Add the vegetable stock, stir, then simmer for 5-10 minutes, until the vegetables are cooked. Check the seasoning, then serve with hot garlic bread (see Cook's Tip).

10 ROASTED HAZELNUT SOUP WITH RED PEPPER CREAM

Preparation time:
30 minutes

Cooking time:
about 30 minutes

Serves 4

Calories:
46 per portion

YOU WILL NEED:

100 g/4 oz hazelnuts, roasted and skins
   removed (see Cook's Tip)

1 onion, chopped

25 g/1 oz butter

450 g/1 lb peeled and diced potatoes

1 garlic clove, crushed

salt and pepper

900 ml/1 ½ pints vegetable stock (see
   recipe 3)

1 tablespoon lemon juice

1 small red pepper

150 ml/ ¼ pint whipping cream

Grate the hazelnuts finely in a food processor or nut mill.

Fry the onion in the butter for 5 minutes, then add the potato, garlic and a little salt and pepper, and cook gently, with a lid on the pan, for a further 5-10 minutes. Pour in the stock, bring to the boil, then simmer for 10-15 minutes, until the potatoes and onions are cooked. Liquidize the soup and stir in the hazelnuts, lemon juice and seasoning to taste.

To make the red pepper cream, put the red pepper under a hot grill until the outer skin is charred all over. Rinse under the cold tap and remove the stalk, seeds and outer skin. Mash the red pepper finely. Whip the cream until just forming peaks, then whisk in enough red pepper to colour the cream pink. Season and serve in individual bowls, with a spoonful of red pepper cream on top.

■ COOK'S TIP

Garlic bread: crush 2-3 garlic cloves and mix into 50 g/2 oz butter. Spread between slices cut across a French stick and bake 15-20 minutes at 180 C/350 F/gas 4.

■ COOK'S TIP

To dry roast nuts, spread them on the bottom of a pan, place over a high flame and shake quickly to keep the contents moving. They are done when slightly brown.

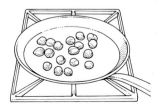

11 CARROT AND CORIANDER SOUP

Preparation time:
15 minutes

Cooking time:
30 minutes

Serves 6

Calories:
105 per portion

YOU WILL NEED:

15 g/½ oz butter or margarine
450 g/1 lb carrots, scraped and sliced
350 g/12 oz leeks, washed and sliced (see Cook's Tip)
1 tablespoon coriander seeds, lightly crushed
zest of ½ lemon
900 ml/1 ½ pints vegetable stock (see recipe 3)
1 tablespoon lemon juice
150 ml/¼ pint single cream
salt and pepper

Melt the butter or margarine in a large saucepan, add the carrots and leeks and fry gently, covered, for 15 minutes, until the vegetables are almost soft. Stir in the coriander seeds and lemon zest and fry for a further 2-3 minutes. Add the vegetable stock, bring to the boil, and simmer for about 10 minutes. Add the lemon juice, cream and seasoning, then blend in a liquidizer or food processor. Reheat and serve.

12 CHILLED CUCUMBER SOUP WITH DILL AND RADISHES

Preparation time:
5 minutes

Serves 4

Calories:
195 per portion

YOU WILL NEED:

1 cucumber, peeled and cut into rough chunks
450 g/16 fl oz thick natural yogurt
2 tablespoons double cream
8 sprigs of mint
2-3 teaspoons white wine vinegar
salt and pepper
FOR THE GARNISH
8 thin slices of radish
4 feathery dill leaves or mint leaves

Put the cucumber into a blender with the yogurt, cream and mint and blend until smooth. Add enough wine vinegar to sharpen the flavour, and salt and pepper to taste. Chill. Serve in chilled bowls garnished with the radish slices and fresh dill or mint leaves.

■ COOK'S TIP

To clean leeks, make a lengthways cut halfway down to the white part of the trimmed leek and hold the leaves open under running water.

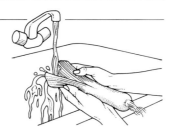

■ COOK'S TIP

Use natural or plain Greek yogurt for this recipe. Greek yogurt has a creamier taste, is thicker and has a higher fat content than ordinary natural yogurt.

13 AUBERGINE DIP

Preparation time:
10 minutes

Cooking time:
about 20 minutes

Serves 4

Calories:
155 per portion

Suitable for vegans

YOU WILL NEED:
2 large aubergines, about 450 g/1 lb
   total
1 small onion, roughly chopped
2 garlic cloves, roughly chopped
4 tablespoons olive oil
2 tablespoons lemon juice
salt and pepper
TO SERVE
1-2 tablespoons chopped fresh parsley
black or green olives
radishes
pitta bread

Thread the aubergines on to a skewer. Place them on the greased grill of a preheated barbecue and cook for 10 minutes, then turn over and cook for a further 10 minutes.

Leave the aubergines until they are cool enough to handle, then peel and chop.

Put the aubergine flesh into a blender or food processor with the remaining ingredients and blend until smooth.

Transfer the purée to a bowl. Sprinkle with the chopped parsley. Serve with olives, radishes and pitta bread.

14 GLOBE ARTICHOKES WITH MINTY YOGURT DRESSING

Preparation time:
40 minutes, plus
cooling

Cooking time:
45 minutes

Serves 4

Calories:
213 per portion

YOU WILL NEED:
4 large globe artichokes (see Cook's
   Tip)
3-4 tablespoons lemon juice
salt
1 tablespoon vegetable oil
sprigs of mint, to garnish
FOR THE DRESSING
300 ml/ 1/2 pint Greek yogurt
1/2 teaspoon lemon zest
1 tablespoon lemon juice
1 tablespoon olive oil
10 cm/4 inch piece cucumber, peeled,
   seeded and grated
2 tablespoons chopped fresh mint
2 hard-boiled eggs, finely chopped
2 spring onions, finely chopped
mint sprigs, to garnish

Cook the artichokes in a pan of boiling, salted water with 1 tablespoon lemon juice added, for 35-45 minutes. When they are tender you will easily be able to pull away the outer leaves. Open out the centre of each artichoke, pull out the tight inner ring of pale leaves and, using a teaspoon, scrape out the prickly centre or 'choke'. Wash and drain the artichokes and leave them to cool for about 1 hour before serving.

Mix all the ingredients for the dressing. Pour into a bowl, garnish with sprigs of mint and serve with the artichokes.

■ COOK'S TIP

Instead of grilling the aubergines on a barbecue, place on a baking tray in a preheated oven 190 C/375 F/ gas 5, for 20-30 minutes until softened. Leave to cool.

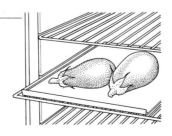

■ COOK'S TIP

To prepare the artichokes brush all the cut surfaces with lemon juice as you prepare them, and drop them into acidulated water. Trim the artichoke stems level with *the base of the leaves and cut off the 2 outside layers of leaves. Cut off the top third of the leaves.*

15 RAW WINTER VEGETABLES WITH SKORDALIA

Preparation time:
45 minutes

Serves 4

Calories:
284 per portion

YOU WILL NEED:
300 ml/ ½ pint low-calorie mayonnaise
25 g/1 oz fresh wholemeal breadcrumbs
25 g/1 oz ground almonds
2 garlic cloves, crushed (or more if you like)
salt and pepper
squeeze of lemon juice
2 tablespoons sesame seeds, toasted
3 tablespoons chopped fresh parsley
2-4 tablespoons natural yogurt (optional)
vegetables (see Cook's Tip)

Make the skordalia. Put the mayonnaise into a bowl and stir in the breadcrumbs and almonds. Add the garlic, salt, pepper and lemon juice. Stir in the sesame seeds and parsley. If the mixture seems a little stiff, add natural yogurt to give a softer consistency.

Taste and adjust the seasoning. Cover and set aside while you prepare the vegetables. Grate the celeriac and carrot, shred the white and red cabbage and thinly slice the broccoli, cauliflower, Brussels sprouts and onions.

Serve clusters of the vegetables on a large platter or in small separate dishes, with the dip in the centre. The dip can be made up to 2 hours in advance, covered and kept at room temperature.

16 ASPARAGUS WITH BUTTER AND LEMON

• **Preparation time:**
5 minutes

Cooking time:
10-15 minutes

Serves 2

Calories:
190 per portion

YOU WILL NEED:
½ bunch asparagus – about 12 pieces
25-50 g/1-2 oz butter
1 tablespoon fresh lemon juice
salt and pepper
lemon wedges

Wash and trim the asparagus, removing the tough stalk ends. Cook in 1 cm/½ inch boiling water or in a steamer saucepan for 10-15 minutes or until the spears feel tender when pierced with the point of a knife. Drain the asparagus then heat the butter and lemon juice in a small saucepan and season with salt and pepper. Serve the asparagus spears immediately with the butter and lemon wedges.

▪ COOK'S TIP

Use about 175 g/6 oz each of: celeriac, carrot, white cabbage, red cabbage, broccoli, cauliflower, Brussels sprouts, peeled onions.

▪ COOK'S TIP

Asparagus should only be lightly cooked. Never buy asparagus that looks woody, wrinkled or dry. Choose a bunch with even-sized spears (the asparagus tips).

17 CHICK PEA PUREE WITH VEGETABLE STICKS

Preparation time:
10 minutes

Cooking time:
about 1 hour

Serves 4

Calories:
195 per portion

YOU WILL NEED:
175 g/6 oz chick peas, soaked overnight
1 bay leaf
1 small bunch of fresh mint
1 teaspoon salt
4 tablespoons lemon juice
2 large garlic cloves, crushed
1 tablespoon olive oil
4 tablespoons natural yogurt
freshly ground black pepper
pinch of paprika
2-3 tablespoons warm water
a selection of fresh vegetable sticks (see
    Cook's Tip)

Drain the chick peas and put them into a pan with the bay leaf and mint; add sufficient water to cover and simmer for 1 hour until tender, adding salt during the last 10 minutes of cooking. Drain and remove bay leaf and mint.

Put the chick peas into a liquidizer with the lemon juice and garlic. Blend until smooth, gradually adding the olive oil and yogurt. Add pepper to taste, the paprika, and a little warm water to adjust consistency.

Serve with a selection of prepared vegetables.

18 MUSHROOM AND RED WINE PATE WITH MELBA TOAST

Preparation time:
10 minutes, plus
chilling

Cooking time:
5 minutes

Serves 6

Calories:
145 per portion

YOU WILL NEED:
50 g/2 oz butter or margarine
750 g/1 ½ lb small firm button
    mushrooms, wiped and thinly sliced
3 tablespoons double cream
1 tablespoon dry red wine
salt and pepper
6-8 slices wholewheat bread for Melba
    toast (see Cook's Tip)

Heat the butter or margarine in a large saucepan and add the mushrooms. Keeping the heat up high, fry the mushrooms quickly for 3-4 minutes, until just tender and lightly browned. If they begin to make liquid, the butter is not hot enough; the mushrooms should be dry. Remove 6 perfect mushroom slices and reserve for garnish. Work the rest in a blender with the cream, red wine and seasoning to taste. Spoon the mixture into 6 individual ramekins or pâté dishes, level the tops, then press one of the reserved mushroom slices into the top of each. Cool, then chill the pâtés.

■ COOK'S TIP

Choose fresh vegetables such as red and green peppers, celery, cucumber, carrots, French beans, spring onions, radishes and broccoli or cauliflower florets.

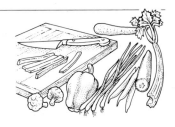

■ COOK'S TIP

To make the Melba toast, first toast the bread on both sides as usual, then with a sharp knife cut through the bread to split each piece in half. Toast the uncooked sides until crisp and brown – the edges will curl up. Allow the toast to cool.

19 FRIED MUSHROOMS KIEV

Preparation time:
about 1 hour, plus
chilling

Cooking time:
about 20 minutes

Serves 4

Calories:
400 per portion

YOU WILL NEED:
24 cup mushrooms
100 g/4 oz unsalted butter, softened
2-3 garlic cloves, crushed
2 tablespoons finely chopped fresh
  parsley
salt and pepper
2 eggs, beaten
75 g/3 oz dried breadcrumbs
vegetable oil, for deep frying
FOR THE GARNISH
chicory leaves
parsley sprigs

Wipe the mushrooms clean with a damp cloth. Carefully pull out the stalks, keeping the caps whole. Chop the stalks finely.

Put the softened butter in a bowl with the chopped mushroom stalks, garlic, parsley, and salt and pepper to taste. Beat together well. Spoon into the mushroom cavities, then sandwich the mushrooms together in pairs. Use wooden cocktail sticks to secure them.

Dip the mushroom pairs one at a time into the beaten egg, then roll in the breadcrumbs. Repeat once more. Chill 1 hour.

Heat the oil in a deep-fat fryer to 190 C/375 F, or until a stale bread cube turns golden in 40-50 seconds. Fry the mushrooms a few at a time for about 5 minutes, turning them frequently with a slotted spoon until golden brown and crisp on all sides. Drain and keep hot while frying the remainder.

Remove the cocktail sticks and serve immediately, garnished with chicory leaves and parsley sprigs.

▪ COOK'S TIP

Mushrooms Kiev are ideal as a starter served with a garlic mayonnaise or yogurt dip (see recipe 30). Alternatively, serve as a main course with a salad and yogurt dressing.

20 TZATZIKI

Preparation time:
10 minutes

Serves 4

Calories:
117 per portion

YOU WILL NEED:
1 cucumber, about 450 g/1 lb, peeled
300 ml/½ pint thick Greek yogurt
2 tablespoons lemon juice
2 tablespoons chopped fresh spring
  onions or chives
2 tablespoons chopped fresh parsley
1 tablespoon chopped fresh mint
1-2 garlic cloves, peeled and crushed, or
  1 shallot, peeled and finely chopped
freshly ground black pepper
large pinch of salt

Chop the cucumber finely.

Mix all the other ingredients together and combine with the cucumber in a serving bowl.

Serve the Tzatziki with warmed wholemeal pitta bread, cut into fingers, and maybe some vegetable crudités (see recipe 17).

▪ COOK'S TIP

This salad is served as a first course in Greece. The cucumber can be exchanged for grated carrot, fennel, celery mixed with apple, Cos lettuce or mushrooms.

21 VEGETABLES A LA GRECQUE

Preparation time:
20 minutes, plus
chilling

Cooking time:
about 10 minutes

Serves 6

Calories:
78 per portion

Suitable for vegans

YOU WILL NEED:
2 tablespoons olive oil
1 large onion, chopped
3 garlic cloves, crushed
1 small-medium cauliflower, trimmed,
*   washed and broken into florets*
350 g/12 oz French beans, trimmed and
*   cut into 2.5 cm/1 inch pieces*
175 g/6 oz button mushrooms, wiped
*   and cut into even-sized pieces*
1 tablespoon coriander seeds, crushed
6 tablespoons lemon juice
salt and pepper
chopped parsley or a few black olives,
*   to garnish*

Heat the oil in a large saucepan, then fry the onion for 5 minutes, without letting it brown. Add the garlic, cauliflower and beans and stir-fry for a further 2-3 minutes, then add the mushrooms and coriander seeds and continue to fry for about 2 minutes, until the mushrooms are beginning to soften. Remove from the heat, add the lemon juice, salt and black pepper to taste. Cool, then chill. Serve on individual plates, sprinkled with chopped parsley and garnished with black olives. Serve with warm rolls or a French stick.

22 HOT STUFFED AVOCADOS

Preparation time:
15 minutes

Cooking time:
15-20 minutes

Oven temperature:
200 C/400 F/gas 6

Serves 8

Calories:
462 per portion

YOU WILL NEED:
4 large ripe avocado pears
zest and juice of 1 well-scrubbed lemon
1 bunch of spring onions, trimmed and
*   chopped*
200 g/7 oz skinned hazelnuts
175 g/6 oz vegetarian Cheddar cheese,
*   grated*
4 tablespoons chopped fresh parsley
4 tablespoons dry white wine
salt and pepper
lemon twists, to garnish

Cut the avocado pears in half and remove the stones. Put the avocado halves, cavity side up, in a shallow casserole dish, then brush the cut surfaces with a little of the lemon juice.

Mix together the onions, hazelnuts, cheese, parsley and wine. Add 2 teaspoons lemon juice and the zest. Season to taste. Divide this mixture between the avocado halves, and bake in a preheated oven for 15-20 minutes, until golden brown.

■ COOK'S TIP

This delicious, lightly-spiced mixture can be made with other vegetables in season. Try replacing the cauliflower with baby Brussels sprouts, quartered, and the French beans with sliced leeks. Carrots would also make a colourful addition.

■ COOK'S TIP

On a ripe avocado, the flesh should yield slightly. If very soft, the avocado is over-ripe. If hard, wrap in paper and leave in a warm place for 2-3 days.

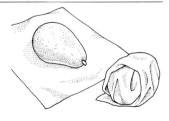

23 CEPES WITH HERB SAUCE

Preparation time:
20 minutes

Cooking time:
about 40 minutes

Serves 6

Calories:
93 per portion

YOU WILL NEED:
40 g/1 ½ oz butter
1 clove garlic, peeled and halved
750 g/1 ½ lb cèpes or other wild
   mushrooms, washed, trimmed and
   cut into bite-sized pieces
1 tablespoon chopped fresh parsley
1 tablespoon chopped fresh chervil
1 tablespoon chopped fresh basil
1 tablespoon plain flour
4 tablespoons dry white wine
150 ml/ ¼ pint double or soured cream
salt and pepper

Melt the butter in a pan. Add the garlic and fry until golden brown. Remove and discard the garlic. Add the cèpes or other mushrooms to the pan and cook over a low heat for about 20 minutes, or until softened.

Add half of the chopped herbs to the pan and mix well. Stir in the flour and cook for 2-3 minutes, stirring well. Gradually add the wine, blending well after each addition to make a smooth sauce. Simmer over a low heat for about 3 minutes. Fold in the double or soured cream and season with salt and pepper to taste. Transfer to a serving dish, sprinkle with the remaining herbs and serve immediately. Serve with French bread and a light, dry white wine.

24 NUT-STUFFED TOMATOES

Preparation time:
20 minutes

Cooking time:
20 minutes

Oven temperature:
180 C/350 F/gas 4

Serves 2

Calories:
312 per portion

YOU WILL NEED:
2 large Mediterranean tomatoes
salt
FOR THE STUFFING
2 tablespoons vegetable oil
75 g/3 oz button mushrooms, finely
   chopped
65 g/2 ½ oz brown rice, cooked (see
   recipe 155)
25 g/1 oz Brazil nuts, coarsely chopped
25 g/1 oz currants
1 teaspoon chopped fresh basil or
   ½ teaspoon dried basil
freshly ground black pepper
FOR THE GARNISH
4 teaspoons soured cream
watercress sprigs

Cut the tomatoes in half and scoop out the pulp. Sprinkle the shells with salt and place in a baking dish.

To prepare the stuffing, heat the oil in a small pan and gently fry the mushrooms for 5 minutes. Stir in the cooked rice, nuts, currants and basil. Add a little salt and plenty of pepper. Spoon the stuffing into the tomato halves.

Cover the dish with foil to keep the stuffing moist and bake for 20 minutes in a preheated oven. Remove from the oven, top each stuffed tomato with a spoonful of soured cream and garnish with watercress. Serve piping hot.

The tomatoes can be prepared up to 8 hours in advance, covered and kept in the refrigerator until needed.

▨ COOK'S TIP

Many unusual varieties of mushrooms are now widely available. Common varieties are Chinese and Japanese mushrooms which are usually sold dried and must be reconstituted in water. Other European varieties include oyster mushrooms, the brown sponge-like morel and the tiny mousserons (all available dried).

▨ COOK'S TIP

As a starter, these are delicious served hot, but they are equally good uncooked for a picnic or cold buffet; serve with salad and French bread to make a light lunch.

25 MUSHROOMS IN HERBED VINAIGRETTE

Preparation time:
5 minutes, plus
chilling

Cooking time:
about 15 minutes

Serves 4

Calories:
140 per portion

Suitable for vegans

YOU WILL NEED:
2 tablespoons walnut oil
2 tablespoons tarragon vinegar
4 tablespoons dry white wine
1 garlic clove, peeled and crushed
salt and pepper
½ teaspoon grated orange zest
1 tablespoon chopped fresh tarragon
1 tablespoon chopped fresh parsley
225 g/8 oz button mushrooms
2 wholemeal pitta breads, cut into
fingers

Put the walnut oil, vinegar, wine and garlic into a shallow pan and add salt and pepper to taste; simmer for 3 minutes. Add the orange zest, tarragon, parsley and mushrooms; cover and simmer for 8 minutes.

Pour the mushrooms and their juices into a shallow dish and allow to cool. Cover and chill for 4 hours. Serve with fingers of warm pitta bread.

■ COOK'S TIP

Mushrooms are great for vegetarians as they are not only very versatile, they have a 'meaty' taste and texture. Mushrooms are best eaten within a day or two of

purchase as they dehydrate very quickly. Store them in a cool place, preferably in a paper bag tucked inside a polythene one.

26 ESTOUFFADE DE BOLETUS

Preparation time:
20 minutes, plus
standing

Cooking time:
about 2 hours

Serves 6

Calories:
111 per portion

Suitable for vegans

YOU WILL NEED:
450 g/1 lb aubergines (see Cook's Tip)
salt
2 tablespoons sunflower oil
350 g/12 oz onions, sliced
3 large garlic cloves, quartered
750 g/1 ½ lb large flat mushrooms,
*   preferably field mushrooms*
2 × 400 g/14 oz cans tomatoes
2 ½ tablespoons tomato purée
1 tablespoon red wine vinegar
1 tablespoon brown sugar
1 tablespoon soy sauce
freshly ground black pepper
2 bay leaves

Heat the oil in a large heavy-based pan and soften the onion and garlic. Slice the mushrooms into strips about 1 cm/½ inch wide.

Rinse the aubergines then squeeze to extract as much liquid as possible. Add the aubergines to the pan. Stir over a medium heat for 1 minute, then add the mushrooms, stir and cover.

Push the tomatoes through a vegetable mill or sieve to remove the seeds and add to the pan. Bring to simmering point, cover and cook for 1 hour, stirring occasionally. Add the remaining ingredients. Stir thoroughly, then continue to simmer uncovered for approximately 45 minutes.

Remove from the heat, cover and leave to stand for 24 hours. Remove the bay leaves. Serve cold, or very slightly warmed, with small wholemeal rolls.

■ COOK'S TIP

To prepare the aubergines, slice into pieces approximately the size of French fries. Transfer to a colander, sprinkle with salt, and set aside to drain.

27 CITRUS REFRESHER WITH MINT SORBET

Preparation time:
20 minutes, plus freezing

Serves 4

Calories:
99 per portion

YOU WILL NEED:
2 large grapefruits
2 large oranges
a little clear honey
FOR THE MINT SORBET
2 tablespoons clear honey
150 ml/5 fl oz water
2 tablespoons finely chopped mint
mint sprigs, to garnish

First, make the sorbet. Mix together the honey, water and mint, then pour into a shallow container and freeze until the mixture is half solid. Break up the mixture with a fork, then freeze until firm.

With a small, serrated knife, and holding the fruit over a bowl, cut all the skin and pith from the grapefruits and oranges. Cut the segments from between the pieces of skin. Sweeten with honey to taste, then divide the fruit between four bowls. Put a spoonful of sorbet on each, decorate with mint, and serve immediately.

28 BLUE CHEESE PEARS

Preparation time:
10 minutes

Serves 4

Calories:
308 per portion

YOU WILL NEED:
100 g/4 oz vegetarian Stilton
225 g/8 oz cottage cheese or curd cheese
2 celery sticks, chopped
50 g/2 oz hazelnuts, chopped
6 large pears
2 tablespoons lemon juice
salad burnet leaves, to garnish

Mash the Stilton, soft cheese and celery together.

Place the chopped nuts in an ungreased heavy-based frying pan over a low heat and stir for 2-3 minutes until slightly browned. Place in a bowl.

Peel and halve the pears and scoop out the cores with a teaspoon. Brush immediately with the lemon juice. Fill the centres of the pears with about half the cheese mixture. Place 3, cut side down, on 4 plates.

With the help of a teaspoon, shape the remaining cheese mixture into 12 balls the size of marbles. Roll each one in the bowl of nuts. Place 3 on each plate. Garnish each plate with salad burnet and serve.

▨ COOK'S TIP

This makes a great starter to get the taste buds going for the main course. It's also low in fat and high in Vitamin C. Try it for breakfast as an ideal wake-me-up.

▨ COOK'S TIP

Vegetarian Stilton, made from vegetarian rennet, is now widely available. Choose curd cheese instead of 'light' soft cheese which may contain gelatine.

BEANS, PULSES & GRAINS

These dishes are all packed with protein and fibre, essential parts of a vegetarian diet. Convenient canned varieties make using pulses and beans quick and easy.

29 VEGETABLE SALAD WITH TARRAGON MAYONNAISE

Preparation time:
45 minutes

Cooking time:
8-10 minutes

Serves 6

Calories:
444 per portion

YOU WILL NEED:
4 medium carrots, cut into thin strips
225 g/8 oz French beans, trimmed
2 leeks, cleaned and cut into rounds
  (see recipe 11)
6 tablespoons unsweetened orange juice
3 tablespoons olive oil
1 garlic clove, crushed
salt and pepper
1 × 425 g/15 oz can black-eyed beans,
  drained and rinsed
175 g/6 oz Brussels sprouts, trimmed,
  washed and finely shredded
10-12 good-shaped spinach leaves
sprigs of fresh tarragon, to garnish
tarragon mayonnaise (see Cook's Tip)

Steam the carrot, beans and leek rounds until just tender – the vegetables should still have a 'bite' to them. Allow to cool.

Mix the orange juice with the olive oil, garlic and salt and pepper to taste; toss the black-eyed beans and the Brussels sprouts in the orange dressing.

Arrange a bed of spinach leaves on each serving plate; spoon the black-eyed beans and shredded sprouts on top.

Arrange the carrots, leeks and beans round the salad. Garnish with sprigs of tarragon and serve as a complete light meal, accompanied by the tarragon mayonnaise.

30 FALAFEL

Preparation time:
10 minutes, plus soaking and resting

Cooking time:
about 20 minutes

Serves 6

Calories:
180 per portion

YOU WILL NEED:
225 g/8 oz chick peas, soaked overnight
4 spring onions
2 cloves garlic, chopped
3 tablespoons water
4 large parsley sprigs
1/2 teaspoon ground cumin
1 teaspoon ground coriander
salt and pepper
vegetable oil for deep frying

Drain the chick peas and place in an electric blender or food processor with the spring onions, garlic, water and parsley. Work to a purée, scraping down the sides when necessary. Stir in the remaining ingredients, with salt and pepper to taste, then turn into a bowl and leave for 1-2 hours to dry out slightly.

Form the mixture into walnut-sized balls and flatten slightly. Heat the oil in a deep-fryer, add the falafel, a few at a time, and fry for about 4 minutes, until golden. Drain.

Serve hot with Tomato yogurt dip (see Cook's Tip).

■ COOK'S TIP

For the tarragon mayonnaise, beat 2 egg yolks with 1 tablespoon lemon juice; gradually whisk in 150 ml/ 1/4 pint olive oil. Blend in 1 crushed garlic clove, *1/2 teaspoon French mustard, 1 1/2 tablespoons chopped fresh tarragon and 4 tablespoons natural yogurt. Season to taste.*

■ COOK'S TIP

For the Tomato yogurt dip, mix together 150 g/5 oz natural yogurt, 1 teaspoon tomato purée, 1 teaspoon ground coriander and 1 teaspoon clear honey.

31 CRACKED WHEAT SALAD

Preparation time:
5 minutes, plus
soaking

Serves 4

Calories:
147 per portion

Suitable for vegans

YOU WILL NEED:
100 g/4 oz bulgur wheat
300 ml/ ½ pint boiling water
2 tablespoons lemon juice
1 tablespoon olive oil
4 tablespoons chopped fresh parsley
4 tablespoons chopped spring onion
2 tablespoons chopped fresh mint
2 tomatoes, skinned and finely chopped
salt and pepper
4 lettuce leaves
FOR THE GARNISH
lemon slices
tomato slices

Put the wheat into a bowl and cover with boiling water. Leave for 10-15 minutes until the wheat has absorbed all the water and puffed up. Add the lemon juice, oil, chopped parsley, spring onion, mint and tomato. Mix well and season to taste. Put two lettuce leaves on two serving plates or in one large bowl, then spoon the salad mixture on top. Garnish with the lemon and tomato slices.

32 BEAN-STUFFED TOMATOES

Preparation time:
20-25 minutes

Cooking time:
15-20 minutes

Oven temperature:
180 C/350 F/gas 4

Serves 4

Calories:
270 per portion

Suitable for vegans

YOU WILL NEED:
1 × 425 g/15 oz can red kidney beans,
  drained
1 small onion, finely chopped
2 tablespoons finely chopped blanched
  almonds (see Cook's Tip)
1 teaspoon chopped fresh sage
1 garlic clove, finely chopped
2 tablespoons wholemeal breadcrumbs
1 small parsnip, peeled and grated
salt and pepper
4 large Mediterranean or 8 medium
  tomatoes
1 tablespoon olive oil

Mix the beans with the onion, almonds, sage, garlic, breadcrumbs, grated parsnip and seasoning.

Cut the tops off the tomatoes and carefully hollow them out. Fill each with the bean mixture. Stand the stuffed tomatoes upright in a lightly greased ovenproof dish. Brush with a little olive oil.

Bake in a preheated oven for 15-20 minutes. Serve with brown rice (see Rice and Pasta chapter for recipes) and a fresh green, leafy salad.

■ COOK'S TIP

This is a traditional Lebanese salad that is quick and easy to prepare. It is based on wheat which has been cracked and steamed. This wheat, called bulgur or burghul, is widely available at supermarkets and only needs soaking. The salad should contain almost as much greenery as wheat.

■ COOK'S TIP

To blanch almonds, drop them into boiling water, bring back to the boil then drain. Squeeze the nuts while warm to slip them out of their skins. Blot dry.

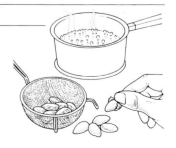

33　CRISP LENTIL PATTIES

Preparation time:
20 minutes

Cooking time:
about 1 hour

Serves 4-6

Calories:
367-244 per portion

YOU WILL NEED:

225 g/8 oz green or brown
　(Continental) lentils, washed
450 ml/¾ pint vegetable stock (see
　recipe 3)
1 tablespoon oil
1 onion, finely sliced
1 green pepper, seeded and finely
　chopped
1 teaspoon ground cumin
1 teaspoon ground coriander
¼ teaspoon chilli powder
salt and pepper
100 g/4 oz jumbo or porridge oats
1 egg, beaten
oil for frying

Place the lentils in a pan with the stock. Bring to the boil and simmer gently until all the stock is absorbed and the lentils are tender, about 40 minutes.

Meanwhile, heat the oil in a pan and fry the onion slowly until cooked but not brown, about 20 minutes. Stir in the pepper and cook for a further 4 minutes then stir in the cumin, coriander, chilli powder, salt and pepper. Add the lentils, mix well and leave to cool. Shape into 8-10 round flat cakes.

Mix the oats with the salt on one plate and pour the beaten egg on to another. Dip each patty first into the egg then into the oats to coat completely. Shallow fry the patties in oil for about 6 minutes, turning once until brown and crisp. Drain.

34　SUNSET STRIPE SALAD

Preparation time:
25 minutes, plus
soaking

Cooking time:
1¼ hours

Serves 4

Calories:
276 per portion

Suitable for vegans

YOU WILL NEED:

175 g/6 oz dried red kidney beans,
　soaked overnight and drained
small bunch of parsley
1 small onion, halved
175 g/6 oz red cabbage, shredded
2 small heads fennel, very thinly sliced
　into rings
2 oranges, segmented
tomato roses (see Cook's Tip)
FOR THE DRESSING
4 tablespoons vegetable oil
½ teaspoon grated orange zest
4 tablespoons orange juice
½ teaspoon fennel seeds, crushed
1 garlic clove, halved
large pinch of mustard powder
salt and pepper

Cook the beans in fast-boiling unsalted water for 15-20 minutes. Add half the parsley and onion and slow boil for about 1 hour, or until just tender. Drain, discard the parsley and onion, run hot water through the beans and drain again.

Meanwhile, mix the dressing ingredients and set aside for about 1 hour. Strain the dressing. Toss the beans in the dressing while they are still hot. Set aside to cool.

In a glass dish, make a layer of the red cabbage, then the fennel, then the orange segments, and cover them with the beans. Cover and set aside for at least 1 hour. Make a pad of parsley sprigs on the salad and place tomato roses on top.

■ COOK'S TIP

Serve the patties with a rich tomato sauce (see recipe 52) and a ribbon pasta, such as tagliatelle or a crunchy salad.

■ COOK'S TIP

To make a tomato rose, choose a firm, slightly under-ripe tomato. Starting at the top and using a sharp knife, peel off a continuous spiral of skin about 1 cm/½ inch wide. With the skin outside, curl the strip into a tight spiral. Arranged on a 'pad' of parsley sprigs, it will look mighty like a rose!

35 THREE BEAN CURRY

Preparation time:
25 minutes

Cooking time:
30-35 minutes

Serves 4

Calories:
485 per portion

**Suitable for vegans
using soya margarine**

YOU WILL NEED:
100 g/4 oz butter or soya margarine
2 medium onions, finely chopped
3 garlic cloves, crushed
1 tablespoon ground coriander
1 teaspoon garam masala powder
1 teaspoon chilli powder
1 × 400 g/14 oz can chopped tomatoes
salt and pepper
1 teaspoon sugar
*1 × 425 g/15 oz can butter beans,
    drained*
*1 × 425 g/15 oz can kidney beans,
    drained*
*1 × 425 g/15 oz can cannellini beans,
    drained*
fresh coriander sprigs, to garnish

Heat the butter in a saucepan, add the onions and fry for 10 minutes until golden brown.

Add the garlic and fry for a few seconds only, then add the coriander, garam masala and chilli powder and stir-fry for a few seconds. Stir in the tomatoes, salt and pepper and sugar. Reduce the heat and cook for 10 minutes.

Add the drained beans, stir thoroughly then cover and cook gently until heated through.

Garnish with the coriander sprigs and serve with poppadums (see Cook's Tip) and a spicy vegetable dish.

36 BEAN AND CABBAGE HOTPOT

Preparation time:
30 minutes, plus
soaking

Cooking time:
1¾ hours

Oven temperature:
220 C/425 F/gas 7

Serves 4

Calories:
379 per portion

**Vegan if butter
omitted**

YOU WILL NEED:
*175 g/6 oz aduki beans, soaked
    overnight in cold water*
1 tablespoon vegetable oil
3 medium onions, chopped
175 g/6 oz carrots, sliced into rings
350 g/12 oz white cabbage, shredded
½ teaspoon celery seed
salt and pepper
900 ml/1½ pints hot vegetable stock
*750 g/1½ lbs potatoes, cooked whole
    in their skins, then sliced*
15 g/½ oz butter or soya margarine
paprika, to garnish

Drain the beans then rinse under cold running water. Put them in a pan, cover with cold water and bring to the boil. Boil fast for 10 minutes, then lower the heat. Half cover the pan and simmer for 35-45 minutes until tender. Drain and rinse.

Heat the oil in a large pan with a lid and cook the onions, carrots and cabbage, covered, for about 5 minutes. Add the celery seed, seasoning and the hot stock. Cover the pan and simmer gently for 15 minutes then stir in the cooked beans.

Spoon the mixture into a large, shallow casserole dish and arrange the slices of potatoes to cover the top. Brush with melted butter or soya margarine and bake near the top of a preheated oven for about 30 minutes until the potatoes are browned and crisp. Sprinkle with paprika before serving.

▦ COOK'S TIP

*Crisp, golden poppadums
make the perfect
accompaniment to curries.
They can be prepared under
the grill, by shallow frying or
deep frying.*

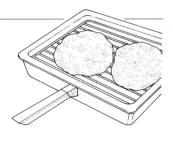

▦ COOK'S TIP

*The sweet-flavoured aduki
bean is peanut-shaped, small
and reddish brown with a
creamy coloured seam. Aduki
beans are low in fat, rich in
fibre, cholesterol-free and an*

*excellent source of protein.
Available from health food
shops, their nutty flavour
blends well with this hotpot.*

37 BEAN AND MUSHROOM SALAD

Preparation time:
15 minutes, plus
soaking

Cooking time:
45 minutes

Serves 6

Calories:
150 per portion

Suitable for vegans

YOU WILL NEED:
*175 g/6 oz black-eyed beans, soaked
   overnight*
salt
100 g/4 oz button mushrooms, sliced
*4 tablespoons French dressing (see
   Cook's Tip)*
1 small red pepper, cored and sliced
2 tablespoons chopped parsley

Drain the beans, place in a pan and cover with cold water. Bring to the boil, cover and simmer for 40-45 minutes until tender, adding a little salt towards the end of the cooking.

Drain thoroughly and place in a bowl with the mushrooms. Pour over the dressing and toss well while still warm. Leave to cool.

Add the red pepper and parsley, toss thoroughly and transfer to a salad bowl.

38 CURRIED BUTTERBEAN SALAD

Preparation time:
12 minutes, plus
soaking

Cooking time:
1 hour 10 minutes

Serves 4

Calories:
286 per portion

YOU WILL NEED:
*350 g/12 oz butterbeans, soaked
   overnight*
2 teaspoons vegetable oil
2 onions, finely chopped
2 teaspoons curry powder
150 ml/¼ pint natural yogurt
1 tablespoon lemon juice
pinch of salt and pepper
½ lettuce, washed (optional)
*1 sprig fresh rosemary to garnish, if
   available*

Drain the butterbeans from their soaking water, put in a large pan, cover with fresh water and bring to the boil. Cover and simmer for 1 hour, or until tender but not broken. Drain.

Heat the oil in a heavy-based pan, add the onions and cook gently for 8 minutes, covering the pan. Add the curry powder and cook for a further 2 minutes.

Meanwhile, mix the yogurt with the lemon juice, salt and pepper. Add this to the onion mixture, then stir in the butterbeans.

To serve, arrange a bed of lettuce on a serving plate, spoon the butterbeans on top and garnish with a sprig of rosemary.

■ COOK'S TIP

*For the French dressing,
place in a screw-topped jar:
5 tablespoons olive oil,
2 tablespoons wine vinegar,
1 teaspoon Dijon mustard,
crushed clove garlic,*   *½ teaspoon honey and salt
and pepper to taste. Shake
well before serving.*

■ COOK'S TIP

*One of Britain's most
popular dried beans, the
butterbean is a member of
the kidney bean family,
though it is much more
subtle in taste.*

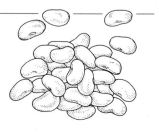

39 LENTIL AND TOMATO SALAD

Preparation time:
15 minutes

Cooking time:
10-15 minutes

Serves 6

Calories:
190 per portion

Suitable for vegans

YOU WILL NEED:
*275 g/10 oz green or Continental
    lentils, washed (see Cook's Tip)*
175 g/6 oz long-grain rice
*6 large tomatoes, peeled, seeded and
    chopped*
1 tablespoon olive oil
2 garlic cloves, finely chopped
1 teaspoon cumin seeds
1 teaspoon black mustard seeds
1 tablespoon vinegar
2 teaspoons lemon juice
salt and pepper

Place the lentils in a large saucepan with plenty of cold water. Do not add salt. Bring to the boil, cover and simmer gently for about 10-12 minutes. When tender, strain and set aside.

Bring a pan of water to the boil and add the rice, simmer for 10-12 minutes then drain, and set aside.

Combine the lentils, rice and tomatoes in a serving bowl. Heat the oil in a frying pan and fry the garlic, cumin and mustard seeds until the garlic is almost burnt; tip over the lentil mixture at once.

Sprinkle over the vinegar and lemon juice, season with salt and pepper and mix thoroughly.

▪ COOK'S TIP

Like red lentils, green or Continental lentils do not need pre-soaking. They hold their shape well when cooked, so are ideal for salads.

40 CHICK PEA AND RED PEPPER SALAD

Preparation time:
15 minutes, plus soaking

Cooking time:
about 2 hours

Serves 4

Calories:
248 per portion

Suitable for vegans

YOU WILL NEED:
*175 g/6 oz chick peas, soaked overnight
    and drained*
2 red peppers
12 black olives
*2 tablespoons chopped fresh coriander
    or parsley*
parsley sprigs, to garnish
FOR THE DRESSING
3 tablespoons vegetable oil
1/2 teaspoon orange zest
2 tablespoons orange juice
1 garlic clove, crushed
salt and pepper

Cook the chick peas in boiling unsalted water for 2 hours, or until they are tender (see Cook's Tip). Drain the chick peas, rinse with hot water and drain them again.

Place the red peppers on a grill rack and cook under a moderate heat for about 20 minutes, turning frequently until the skins are black and blistered. Hold the peppers under cold water then, using a small, sharp knife, peel off the skins. Halve the peppers, remove the core and seeds and thinly slice.

Mix together the dressing ingredients. Toss the chick peas in the dressing while still hot. Set aside to cool. Stir in the peppers, olives and half the coriander or parsley. Turn the salad into a serving dish and sprinkle with the remaining coriander or parsley and garnish with parsley sprigs.

▪ COOK'S TIP

Chick peas that have been kept for a long time will take longer to cook. Buy chick peas in small quantities and store in an airtight jar in a cool, dry place.

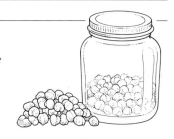

41 GREEK BEAN SALAD

Preparation time:
15 minutes, plus
soaking

Cooking time:
1¼ hours

Serves 4

Calories:
437 per portion

YOU WILL NEED:

250 g/9 oz dried black-eyed or white
    haricot beans, soaked overnight in
    cold water
1 litre/¾ pint water
salt
cayenne pepper
4 tomatoes, diced
2 large onions, chopped
100 g/4 oz feta cheese, cured
FOR THE DRESSING
2 garlic cloves, crushed with salt
2 tablespoons wine vinegar
4 tablespoons olive oil
½ teaspoon chopped fresh oregano

Drain the beans and place in a pan with the water. Bring slowly to the boil, then lower the heat and cook gently for about 1 hour. Season to taste with salt and cayenne pepper and cook for a further 10-20 minutes, until just tender. Drain in a sieve and leave to cool.

Place the beans in a large serving bowl and mix with the tomatoes, onion and cheese.

To make the dressing, beat the garlic with the vinegar, olive oil and oregano. Pour over the salad and toss to mix. Leave to stand for 10-15 minutes to allow the flavours to develop. Toss again before serving.

42 LENTIL AND MUSHROOM GRATIN

Preparation time:
30 minutes

Cooking time:
about 1½ hours

Oven temperature:
190 C/375 F/gas 5

Serves 4

Calories:
397 per portion

YOU WILL NEED:

2 tablespoons oil
1 onion, chopped
1 carrot, chopped
2 celery sticks, chopped
1 garlic clove, crushed
225 g/8 oz red lentils
600 ml/1 pint water
2 tablespoons soy sauce
salt and pepper
FOR THE MUSHROOM FILLING
25 g/1 oz margarine
225 g/8 oz flat mushrooms, sliced
2 garlic cloves, crushed
3 tablespoons chopped parsley
75 g/3 oz vegetarian Cheddar, grated

Heat the oil in a pan, add the onion, carrot and celery and fry gently for 10 minutes, until softened. Add the remaining ingredients, with salt and pepper to taste. Cover and simmer for 50-60 minutes, stirring occasionally, until tender.

For the filling, melt the margarine in a frying pan, add the mushrooms and fry for 2 minutes, stirring. Add the garlic, parsley, and salt and pepper to taste and mix well.

Place half the lentil mixture in an oiled ovenproof dish. Spread the mushrooms over the top, then cover with the remaining lentil mixture. Top with the cheese and bake in a preheated oven for 20-25 minutes until golden.

■ COOK'S TIP

*This salad can be served as
part of a cold buffet for
parties or picnics, or with a
wholemeal roll for lunch.
If fresh oregano isn't
available, use parsley.*

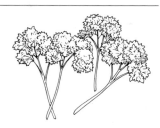

■ COOK'S TIP

*Red lentils are ideal for
soups and stews as they are
quick cooking and do not
require pre-soaking. As they
lose their shape when
cooked, do not use in salads.*

43   PROVENCALE BEAN STEW

Preparation time:
15 minutes, plus
soaking

Cooking time:
2-2¼ hours

Serves 4

Calories:
344 per portion

Suitable for vegans

YOU WILL NEED:
350 g/12 oz haricot beans or pinto
    beans, soaked overnight
salt and pepper
2 tablespoons olive oil
2 onions, sliced
1 red pepper, cored, seeded and sliced
1 green pepper, cored, seeded and sliced
2 garlic cloves, crushed
1 × 397 g/14 oz can chopped tomatoes
2 tablespoons tomato purée
1 bouquet garni
50 g/2 oz black olives, halved and
    stoned
2 tablespoons chopped parsley

Drain the beans, place in a pan and cover with cold water. Bring to the boil, boil for 10 minutes, then cover and simmer for 1-1¼ hours, until almost tender, adding a pinch of salt towards the end of cooking. Drain, reserving 300 ml/½ pint of the liquid.

Heat the oil in a pan, add the onions and fry until softened. Add the peppers and garlic and fry gently for 10 minutes. Add the tomatoes with their juice, tomato purée, beans, reserved liquid, bouquet garni and salt and pepper to taste. Cover and simmer for 45 minutes, adding the olives and parsley 5 minutes before the end of the cooking time. Remove the bouquet garni.

Serve with garlic bread and salad.

▦ COOK'S TIP

Never add salt to dried beans during the early stages of cooking – it will make the skins tough and prevent the beans becoming tender. Add salt (not too much) during *the last 10 minutes of the calculated cooking time.*

44   MULTI-COLOURED BEAN SALAD

Preparation time:
15 minutes, plus
marinating

Serves 6

Calories:
325 per portion

Suitable for vegans

YOU WILL NEED:
1 × 225 g/8 oz can chick peas, drained
1 × 225 g/8 oz can red kidney beans,
    drained
1 × 255 g/8 oz can white kidney beans,
    drained
225 g/8 oz cooked French beans,
    chopped into 2.5 cm/1 inch lengths
1 red pepper, cored, seeded and finely
    sliced
1 bunch spring onions, chopped
2 garlic cloves, peeled
½ teaspoon salt
2 tablespoons tahini
1 tablespoon lemon juice
1 tablespoon soy sauce
2 tablespoons water
1 tablespoon chopped fresh parsley or
    coriander

Rinse all the canned beans. Combine with the French beans, red pepper and spring onions in a deep serving bowl.

Crush the garlic with the salt and combine with the tahini, lemon juice, soy sauce and water. If the dressing is too thick, add a little more water. Stir the dressing into the beans and sprinkle the parsley or coriander over.

Leave to marinate for 2 hours before serving as part of a picnic, buffet, or light lunch snack.

▦ COOK'S TIP

Tahini (sesame seed paste), combined with the beans, means a complete protein is obtained. Red pepper also increases the vitamin C content.

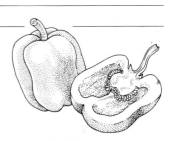

45 VEGETARIAN HOTPOT

Preparation time:
15 minutes, plus
soaking

Cooking time:
2-2¼ hours

Serves 2

Calories:
420 per portion

YOU WILL NEED:
25 g/1 oz dried chick peas
25 g/1 oz dried haricot beans
25 g/1 oz dried black-eyed beans
25 g/1 oz dried red kidney beans
15 g/½ oz butter
1 small onion, chopped
1 carrot, sliced
1 celery stick, chopped
1 garlic clove, crushed
1 × 227 g/8 oz can tomatoes
½ teaspoon dried mixed herbs
salt and pepper
75 g/3 oz vegetarian Cheddar, grated

Place the chick peas, haricot beans and black-eyed beans in a bowl and cover with cold water. Place the kidney beans in a separate bowl and cover with water. Soak overnight.

Drain and place the chick peas, haricot beans and black-eyed beans in a saucepan; put the kidney beans in a separate pan (to avoid tinting the others pink). Cover the pulses with fresh cold water. Bring to the boil, boil for 10 minutes, then cover and simmer for 40 minutes or until tender. Drain, rinse under cold water, then drain thoroughly.

Melt the butter in a saucepan, add the onion, carrot and celery and fry until soft. Stir in the garlic, pulses, tomatoes with their juice, herbs, and salt and pepper to taste.

Bring to the boil, cover and simmer for 1-1¼ hours, adding a little water if the mixture becomes too dry. Sprinkle with the cheese. Serve with rice (see Cook's Tip).

46 BANANA MUESLI

Preparation time:
15 minutes, plus
soaking

Serves 4

Calories:
285 per portion

YOU WILL NEED:
100 g/4 oz rolled oats
50 g/2 oz sunflower seeds
300 ml/½ pint water
2 tablespoons clear honey
2 large bananas, peeled and sliced
225 g/8 oz black grapes, halved and
    de-seeded
grated zest of 1 large well-scrubbed
    orange, and 1 large, well-scrubbed
    lemon
50 g/2 oz flaked almonds, toasted

Put the rolled oats and sunflower seeds into a bowl with the water; leave to soak overnight if possible (see Cook's Tip). Mix well until creamy, and add the honey, bananas, grapes and orange and lemon zest. Spoon into a large serving dish or four small ones and sprinkle with toasted almond flakes.

▣ COOK'S TIP

To cook long-grain rice, place the rice in a pan with double its volume in water. Bring to the boil, cover and simmer for 20 minutes. By the end of the cooking time the rice grains will have absorbed all the water and be dry and separate. Simply fluff with a fork and serve.

▣ COOK'S TIP

Soaking the oats overnight in water gives the muesli extra creaminess. If you also soak the sunflower seeds, they will begin to germinate, adding extra health-giving enzymes.

47 TWO-BEAN VEGETABLE GOULASH

Preparation time:
30 minutes, plus
soaking

Cooking time:
1 hour 20 minutes

Serves 4

Calories:
352 per portion

**Omit soured cream
for vegans**

YOU WILL NEED:
*100 g/4 oz each black-eyed and
   cannellini beans, soaked overnight
   (see Cook's Tip)*
1 tablespoon vegetable oil
*100 g/4 oz very small onions, or
   shallots, peeled but left whole*
4 sticks of celery, sliced into chunks
4 small courgettes, cut in chunks
3 small carrots, cut in chunks
1 × 400 g/14 oz can tomatoes
300 ml/½ pint vegetable stock
1 tablespoon paprika
½ teaspoon caraway seeds
salt and pepper
1 tablespoon cornflour
2 tablespoons water

Heat the oil in a large pan and fry the onions, celery, courgettes and carrots quickly over a high heat until lightly browned. Pour in the tomatoes with their juice and the stock. Stir in the paprika, caraway seeds, salt and pepper. Cover and simmer for 20 minutes until the vegetables are tender.

Stir both lots of cooked beans into the vegetables. Blend the cornflour with the water and add to the pan. Bring to the boil, stirring, until the sauce thickens a little. Cover the pan and simmer again for about 10 minutes. Spoon the goulash into a warmed dish and serve with soured cream, if liked.

▦ COOK'S TIP

Drain the beans and rinse under cold running water. Put them in two separate pans, cover with water and bring to the boil. Boil fast for 10 minutes then lower
the heat, half cover the pans and simmer for about 1 hour until tender. Drain, rinse and set aside.

48 BLACKBERRY AND APPLE MUESLI

Preparation time:
10 minutes

Serves 4

Calories:
340 per portion

Suitable for vegans

YOU WILL NEED:
8 tablespoons porridge oats
2 tablespoons jumbo oats
1 tablespoon bran
1 tablespoon sunflower seeds
4 tablespoons mixed chopped nuts
4 tablespoons sultanas
2 dessert apples, cored and thinly sliced
1 tablespoon lemon juice
225 g/8 oz blackberries
natural yogurt or buttermilk, to serve

Mix together the porridge oats, jumbo oats, bran, sunflower seeds, nuts and sultanas. Toss the sliced apple in the lemon juice.

Spoon the muesli mixture into 4 cereal bowls, arrange the apple slices in a ring around the outside and pile the blackberries in the centre. Serve with natural yogurt or buttermilk for breakfast or a family supper.
Note: For vegans, replace the yogurt or buttermilk with soya milk.

▦ COOK'S TIP

You can make the muesli mix of the cereals, seeds, nuts and dried fruits in larger quantities and store in an airtight container in a cool, dry place.

49 BLACK-EYED BEAN BAKE

Preparation time:
15 minutes, plus
soaking

Cooking time:
2 hours 10 minutes

Oven temperature:
180 C/350 F/gas 4

Serves 4

Calories:
491 per portion

**Suitable for vegans
without the Cheddar**

YOU WILL NEED:

225 g/8 oz dried black-eyed beans,
    soaked for at least 1 hour
3 tablespoons olive oil
1 large onion, chopped
2 potatoes, peeled and sliced
2 large carrots, chopped
2 turnips, diced
2 parsnips, diced
2 celery sticks, chopped
1 tablespoon chopped fresh parsley
1 tablespoon dried thyme
1 teaspoon dried oregano
2 bay leaves
salt and pepper
1 teaspoon black treacle
2 tablespoons tomato purée
50 g/2 oz vegetarian Cheddar, grated

Cook the beans (see Cook's Tip). Meanwhile, heat the oil in a flameproof casserole, add the onion and fry until softened. Stir in the vegetables. Cover and cook over a gentle heat for 10 minutes.

Drain the beans, reserving their cooking liquid. Stir the beans into the casserole with the herbs and salt and pepper. Pour over 600 ml/1 pint of the cooking liquid, to cover the vegetables. Stir in the black treacle and tomato purée. Cover tightly and transfer to a preheated oven for 1½ hours.

Uncover the casserole and discard the bay leaves. Sprinkle over the cheese. Cook without a lid for a further 10 minutes.

■ COOK'S TIP

Put the beans and their soaking water in a large saucepan. Bring to the boil and fast boil for 10 minutes, then cover and simmer gently for 20 minutes.

50 BROAD BEAN SALAD

Preparation time:
15 minutes

Cooking time:
10-12 minutes

Serves 4

Calories:
86 per portion

YOU WILL NEED:

450 g/1 lb fresh or frozen broad beans,
    shelled weight
1-2 teaspoons chopped fresh summer
    savory, dill or tarragon
4 spring onions, trimmed and finely
    chopped
1 tablespoon horseradish sauce
150 ml/¼ pint natural yogurt
pinch of salt and pepper
sprig of fresh summer savory, dill or
    tarragon, to garnish

If using fresh beans, plunge them into 1 cm/½ inch boiling water in a saucepan. Bring back to the boil, cover and simmer for 10-12 minutes. If using frozen beans, cook according to the instructions on the packet. Drain.

Mix all the other ingredients for the salad together in a serving dish.

Toss the warm beans in the dressing. Taste, and add a little more horseradish or salt if necessary. Serve immediately, garnished with a sprig of summer savory, dill or tarragon.

■ COOK'S TIP

If you are able to buy fresh horseradish, use ½-1 teaspoon of finely grated horseradish instead of the horseradish sauce.

51 MEXICAN REFRIED BEANS

Preparation time:
5 minutes, plus soaking

Cooking time:
about 2½ hours

Serves 8

Calories:
267 per portion

Suitable for vegans

YOU WILL NEED:
450 g/1 lb dried black-eyed, pinto or
*   red kidney beans, soaked overnight*
*   and drained*
1 medium onion, diced
1 garlic clove, crushed
1.2 litres/2 pints water
100 g/4 oz white vegetable fat
pinch chilli powder
salt

Put the beans in a large pan with the onion, garlic and water. Bring to the boil and fast boil for 10 minutes, then lower the heat and simmer until the beans are tender – about 2 hours. Add more water if necessary.

Drain, reserving some of the liquid. Lightly mash the beans with a fork – do not purée.

Heat the fat in a wide, heavy frying pan and add the chilli powder and mashed beans. Cook, stirring and turning until the beans are thickened and the fat is absorbed. Salt to taste. Add a little of the reserved bean liquid if they look dry.

■ COOK'S TIP

Refried beans are ideal with taco shells. Simply heat the shells in the oven, fill with the beans and top with salad, salsa sauce, soured cream and cheese.

52 LENTIL AND WATERCRESS PATTIES

Preparation time:
30 minutes

Cooking time:
50 minutes

Serves 6

Calories:
423 per portion

Suitable for vegans

YOU WILL NEED:
3 tablespoons vegetable oil
1 large onion, finely chopped
1 garlic clove, crushed
225 g/8 oz split red lentils
600 ml/1 pint vegetable stock
few parsley stalks
2 tablespoons tomato purée
100 g/4 oz blanched almonds, chopped
1 bunch watercress, finely chopped
1 tablespoon chopped fresh mint
salt and pepper
2 tablespoons plain flour
oil for frying

Heat the oil in a medium pan and fry the onion and garlic over a moderate heat for 2 minutes, stirring once or twice. Add the lentils and stir to coat them with oil. Pour on the stock, add the parsley stalks and bring to the boil. Lower the heat, cover the pan and simmer for 40 minutes. The lentils should be soft and the stock absorbed – increase the heat to evaporate any left. Discard the parsley and remove the pan from the heat.

Beat the lentils with a wooden spoon and stir in the tomato purée, almonds, watercress and mint. Season. Divide the mixture into 12 and mould into 'burger' shapes. Toss in the flour to coat them thoroughly. Fry the patties in hot oil over a moderate heat for about 5 minutes on each side, or until they are crisp. Serve with Tomato sauce (see Cook's Tip).

■ COOK'S TIP

For the Tomato sauce, heat 2 tablespoons olive oil in a pan, add a chopped onion and sauté for 5 minutes. Stir in a 400 g/14 oz can chopped tomatoes, 150 ml/ ¼ pint vegetable stock (see recipe 3), 2 teaspoons tomato purée and salt and pepper to taste. Simmer for 30 minutes.

MAIN COURSES

These dishes make the most of all varieties of vegetables, bringing out their subtle but distinctive flavours and making the best use of their valuable vitamins, minerals and fibre. Choose vegetables in season and prepare them just before serving to retain as much as possible of their nutritional content.

53   SPINACH PANCAKES

Preparation time:
25 minutes, plus standing

Cooking time:
about 25 minutes

Oven temperature:
190 C/375 F/gas 5

Serves 4

Calories:
472 per portion

YOU WILL NEED:
100 g/4 oz wholemeal flour
1 egg, beaten
300 ml/ ½ pint milk
FOR THE FILLING
350 g/12 oz frozen, chopped spinach
175 g/6 oz Ricotta cheese
2 tablespoons grated Parmesan cheese
1 egg
salt and pepper
grated nutmeg

Cheese sauce (see Cook's Tip)
1 tablespoon grated Parmesan cheese
1 tablespoon wholemeal breadcrumbs

Make and cook the pancakes as for Pancakes with Celery and Peanuts (recipe 54).

For the filling, place the spinach in a pan and heat gently until completely thawed. Cook for 2 minutes, then pour off any liquid. Beat in the cheeses, egg, salt, pepper and nutmeg to taste. Divide the filling between the pancakes, roll up and place in an oiled, shallow ovenproof dish.

Make the Cheese sauce.

Spoon the sauce over the pancakes, then sprinkle with the Parmesan cheese and breadcrumbs. Cook in a preheated moderately hot oven for 15-20 minutes, until golden.

54   PANCAKES WITH CELERY AND PEANUTS

Preparation time:
25 minutes, plus standing

Cooking time:
about 25 minutes

Serves 4

Calories:
203 per portion

YOU WILL NEED:
50 g/2 oz wholemeal flour
pinch of salt
1 egg
150 ml/ ¼ pint skimmed milk and water mixed
1 tablespoon chopped fresh parsley
olive oil
FOR THE FILLING
6 celery sticks, coarsely chopped
100 g/4 oz button mushrooms, chopped
50 g/2 oz unsalted, skinned peanuts, roughly chopped
½ teaspoon dried oregano
freshly ground black pepper
2 tablespoons chopped fresh parsley

Mix the flour and salt in a bowl; make a well in the centre, and add the egg and the milk plus water. Beat until smooth and stir in the parsley. Cover and leave for 20 minutes.

Heat 1 tablespoon of oil in a frying pan and fry the celery for 3-4 minutes. Add the mushrooms, peanuts, oregano and pepper and cook for 4-5 minutes. Stir in the parsley.

Brush the base of a small frying pan with oil. When hot, add sufficient batter to thinly cover the base; cook until golden on both sides. Cook 7 more pancakes.

Divide the filling between the pancakes, roll them up and serve, garnished with parsley, if liked.

▮ COOK'S TIP

Cheese sauce: heat 2 tablespoons oil, stir in 2 tablespoons wholemeal flour, off the heat. Blend in 300 ml/ ½ pint milk and bring to the boil, stirring, *until thickened. Take off the heat and stir in 50 g/2 oz grated vegetarian Cheddar cheese.*

▮ COOK'S TIP

Don't worry if the pancake batter has lumps. Simply push it through a sieve into a clean bowl for smooth results.

55 PANCAKES WITH RED PEPPER AND TOMATO FILLING

Preparation time:
30 minutes, plus standing

Cooking time:
1 hour 10 minutes

Oven temperature:
190 C/375 F/gas 5

Serves 4

Calories:
442 per portion

YOU WILL NEED:
8 pancakes (see recipe 54)
750 g/1 ½ lb sweet red peppers
2 tablespoons olive oil
1 onion, chopped
1 ½ kg/3 lb tomatoes, skinned, seeded and chopped
salt and pepper
300 ml/ ½ pint soured cream or thick Greek yogurt
paprika

First make the filling. Heat the red peppers under a hot grill until they're browned all over, and the outer skins will come off easily. Put the peppers into cold water and peel off the skins. Remove the stalk ends and seeds and cut into small pieces. Heat the oil in a large saucepan and fry the onion for 10 minutes, then put in the peppers and tomatoes and cook, uncovered, for about 30 minutes, until the mixture is fairly thick and dry. Stir frequently to prevent burning. Season to taste.

Make and cook the pancakes.

To assemble the dish, put a spoonful of the pepper and tomato mixture on each pancake and roll up neatly. Place the pancakes in a shallow ovenproof dish. Give the cream a quick stir, then spoon over the pancakes. Sprinkle with paprika and cover with foil. Place in a preheated oven and bake for about 20 minutes, until heated through. Serve at once.

■ COOK'S TIP

Pancakes can be made in advance and deep-frozen. To freeze the pancakes, stack them up on top of each other with a layer of greaseproof paper between each one.

Allow to cool, then pack in a polythene bag. Defrost and bake the pancakes for about 10-15 minutes until hot through.

56 TOMATO-STUFFED PANCAKES

Preparation time:
45 minutes

Cooking time:
1½ hours

Oven temperature:
190 C/375 F/gas 5

Serves 4

Calories:
500 per portion

YOU WILL NEED:
8 pancakes (see recipe 54)
FOR THE FILLING
25 g/1 oz butter
½ onion, finely chopped
4 tomatoes, skinned and chopped
100 g/4 oz mushrooms, chopped
1 teaspoon mixed herbs
25 g/1 oz fresh white breadcrumbs
salt and pepper
FOR THE TOPPING
40 g/1 ½ oz butter
40 g/1 ½ oz plain flour
300 ml/ ½ pint milk
75 g/3 oz vegetarian Cheddar, grated

Make the pancakes. For the filling, melt the butter in a medium pan and fry the onion, tomatoes and mushrooms until reduced to a pulp. Stir in the herbs and breadcrumbs and season well. Divide the filling between the pancakes and roll them up. Arrange side by side in an ovenproof dish.

To make the topping, melt the butter in a heavy pan, remove from the heat and stir in the flour. Gradually beat in the milk, then return to the heat and bring to the boil, stirring constantly. Simmer for 3-4 minutes, stirring. Stir 50 g/2 oz of the cheese into the white sauce, season and pour over the pancakes. Sprinkle over the remaining cheese. Bake in a preheated oven for 30 minutes until golden brown.

■ COOK'S TIP

Instead of the fresh tomatoes, use a 200 g/7 oz can of chopped tomatoes. Add 1 tablespoon of freshly chopped basil instead of the mixed herbs, if liked.

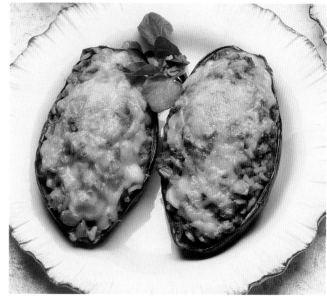

57 WINTER STEW

Preparation time:	YOU WILL NEED:
30 minutes	2-3 tablespoons vegetable oil
	1 large onion, chopped
Cooking time:	5-6 root vegetables (carrots, parsnips
1½ hours	etc), in bite-size pieces
	2 leeks, halved, washed and sliced
Oven temperature:	3 potatoes, peeled, cut in chunks
200 C/400 F/gas 6	1 tablespoon plain white flour
	1.2 litres/2 pints hot vegetable stock
Serves 4	1 tablespoon tomato purée
Calories:	¼ teaspoon celery seeds
392 per portion	salt and pepper
Suitable for vegans	dumplings (see Cook's Tip)
using soya margarine	1 tablespoon chopped parsley

Heat a little of the oil in a pan, and fry the onion quickly until golden brown. Transfer to an ovenproof casserole. Adding a little more oil as necessary, brown the vegetables in batches then transfer to the casserole. Add a little more oil to the pan, stir in the flour, and cook over a steady heat, stirring, until the flour is browned. Pour in the stock and bring to the boil, stirring, until the stock has thickened. Add the purée, celery seeds, salt and pepper, then pour over the vegetables. Cover the casserole and cook in a preheated oven for 50 minutes. Meanwhile, make the dumplings.

When the casserole has cooked 50 minutes, remove the lid and add the dumplings. Replace the lid and put back into the oven for a further 20-30 minutes. The dumplings will rise to the top and swell to double their size. Serve the stew hot, garnished with parsley.

■ COOK'S TIP

For the dumplings, rub 25 g/1 oz vegetable or soya margarine into 175 g/6 oz wholemeal self-raising flour. Add teaspoon dried mixed herbs and seasoning. Mix to a soft dough with 1 tablespoon vegetable oil and 8 tablespoons water. Shape into 8 balls.

58 WALNUT-STUFFED AUBERGINES

Preparation time:	YOU WILL NEED:
30 minutes	2 large aubergines
	2 tablespoons olive oil
Cooking time:	1 onion, chopped
40 minutes	2 garlic cloves, crushed
	3 celery sticks, chopped
Oven temperature:	175 g/6 oz mushrooms, chopped
190 C/375 F/gas 5	6 tablespoons brown rice, cooked (see
	recipe 155)
Serves 4	50 g/2 oz walnuts, ground
Calories:	1 tablespoon tomato purée
248 per portion	2 tablespoons chopped parsley
	salt and pepper
	75 g/3 oz vegetarian Cheddar cheese,
	grated

Prick the aubergines all over, cut in half and place cut side down on a greased baking sheet. Bake in a preheated oven for 30 minutes.

Meanwhile, heat the oil in a pan, add the onion and fry until softened. Add the garlic and celery and fry for 5 minutes. Add the mushrooms and cook, stirring, for 3 minutes. Stir in the rice, walnuts, tomato purée, parsley, and seasoning. Turn off the heat.

Scoop the flesh from the aubergines, without breaking the skins, chop finely and mix with the fried mixture. Pile into the aubergine skins, sprinkle with the cheese and heat under a hot grill until bubbling. Serve with a crisp, mixed salad.

■ COOK'S TIP

To scoop out the flesh of an aubergine, halve it and criss-cross through each half with a sharp knife without penetrating the skin. Carefully cut out the flesh.

59 HOT BOSTON BEANS

Preparation time:
20 minutes, plus
soaking

Cooking time:
2¾ hours

Oven temperature:
150 C/300 F/gas 2

Serves 4

Calories:
303 per portion

YOU WILL NEED:
*225 g/8 oz haricot beans, soaked
    overnight in cold water*
1 tablespoon vegetable oil
2 medium onions, chopped
4 tablespoons clear honey
3 tablespoons soy sauce
½ teaspoon Tabasco sauce
3 tablespoons wine vinegar
1 teaspoon English mustard powder
½-1 teaspoon ground chilli
1 teaspoon paprika
4 tablespoons tomato purée
450 ml/¾ pint hot vegetable stock
4 tablespoons orange juice
2 teaspoons plain wholemeal flour
2 tablespoons water
2 red peppers, seeded and sliced

Rinse the beans and put in a pan with water to cover. Bring to
the boil and simmer 30 minutes. Drain. Tip into a casserole.

Heat the oil in a large pan and gently fry the onions until
golden. Stir in the honey, soy sauce, Tabasco sauce, vinegar,
mustard, chilli, paprika and tomato purée.

Pour in the hot stock and orange juice and bring to the boil.
Pour over the beans, cover the casserole and cook in the centre
of a preheated oven for 1½ hours.

Blend the flour with the water and stir into the beans. Add
the red peppers. Cover and return to the oven for 1 hour until
the sauce is rich and thick and the beans tender.

■ COOK'S TIP

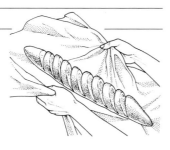

*The dish can be prepared up
to 24 hours in advance and
kept covered and chilled.
Reheat in the oven for about
an hour. Serve it with lots of
hot garlic bread (recipe 9).*

60 STUFFED VEGETABLES

Preparation time:
40 minutes

Cooking time:
20-25 minutes

Oven temperature:
200 C/400 F/gas 6

Serves 4

Calories:
483 per portion

Suitable for vegans

YOU WILL NEED:
2 medium aubergines
2 large courgettes
2 large Mediterranean tomatoes
4 large flat field mushrooms
vegetable oil, for brushing
1 tablespoon vegetable oil
1 garlic clove, crushed
1 large onion, chopped
100 g/4 oz mushrooms, chopped
200 g/7 oz wholemeal breadcrumbs
2 tablespoons chopped fresh basil
½ teaspoon yeast extract

Trim the aubergines and courgettes and halve lengthways.
Hollow out the centres and cut the flesh into small pieces.
Blanch the shells in boiling water for 2 minutes, then drain and
set aside. Cut the tomatoes in half and scoop the flesh and seeds
into a bowl. Trim the stalks from the mushrooms and reserve.
Brush all the vegetable cases with oil, inside and out, and
arrange in 2 roasting tins.

Heat the oil in a pan and fry the garlic and onion until
golden brown. Chop the reserved mushroom stalks and add
them together with the mushrooms, breadcrumbs, basil, yeast
extract, aubergine and courgette pieces and the tomato flesh.
Mix the stuffing, season and spoon into the prepared vegetable
cases. Pour 2-3 tablespoons of water into each roasting tin and
bake in a preheated oven for about 20 minutes.

Lift the vegetables carefully on to a warm serving dish and
sprinkle over the garnish (see Cook's Tip).

■ COOK'S TIP

*For the garnish, heat
2 teaspoons vegetable oil in a
small pan, then add
2 tablespoons pumpkin
seeds. Fry for 1-2 minutes
until browned. Drain on*
*absorbent kitchen paper, cool
and mix with 1 tablespoon
chopped fresh parsley.*

61 SAVOURY NUT ROAST

Preparation time:
30 minutes

Cooking time:
50 minutes

Oven temperature:
180 C/350 F/gas 4

Serves 4

Calories:
618 per portion

Suitable for vegans using soya margarine

YOU WILL NEED:
50 g/2 oz butter or soya margarine
2 large onions, finely chopped
100 g/4 oz cashew nuts, grated, or
    100 g/4 oz peanuts, grated
100 g/4 oz hazelnuts or almonds,
    grated
100 g/4 oz soft wholewheat
    breadcrumbs
1 tablespoon chopped mixed herbs
1-2 teaspoons yeast extract
salt and pepper
sprigs of parsley, to garnish

Grease a 20 cm/8 inch square tin or shallow casserole dish. Melt the fat in a large saucepan and fry the onions gently for 10 minutes, until tender. Then add the nuts, breadcrumbs, herbs, yeast extract and salt and pepper to taste. Press into the prepared tin or casserole dish and smooth the top. Bake in a preheated oven for 35-40 minutes. Ease the nut roast out of the tin or casserole; cut it into wedges and serve these on individual plates or arrange them on a warmed serving dish with vegetables and garnished with sprigs of parsley if wished. Serve with vegetarian sherry gravy (see Cook's Tip) and vegetables.

62 COUSCOUS WITH SPICED VEGETABLE STEW

Preparation time:
25 minutes

Cooking time:
45 minutes

Serves 4

Calories:
725 per portion

YOU WILL NEED:
350 g/12 oz couscous
1/2 teaspoon salt dissolved in 600 ml/
    1 pint warm water
4 tablespoons olive oil
2 onions, peeled and chopped
450 g/1 lb carrots, sliced
2 teaspoons each cinnamon, ground
    cumin and ground coriander
100 g/4 oz raisins
2 × 400 g/14 oz cans chick peas,
    drained, or 450 g/1 lb frozen beans,
    peas or sweetcorn
900 ml/1 1/2 pints water
4 tablespoons tomato purée
salt and pepper
2 tablespoons chopped parsley
lemon wedges, for garnish

Place the couscous in a bowl. Add the water and set aside. Heat half the oil in the saucepan part of a steamer. Add the onion and carrots and fry gently for 10 minutes. Add the spices and cook for 2-3 minutes, stirring. Put in the raisins and the chosen pulse, water and tomato purée. Bring to the boil, and reduce the heat so the stew just simmers. Now put the couscous into the top part of the steamer, over the stew. Cover and steam 25-30 minutes. Season to taste. Stir the remaining oil and parsley into the couscous. Garnish with lemon wedges.

■ COOK'S TIP

For the gravy, put 300 ml/ 1 pint vegetable stock (see recipe 3), 1 1/2 teaspoons soy sauce and 1 tablespoon redcurrant jelly into a pan and bring to the boil. Blend

1 1/2 teaspoons cornflour with 1 1/2 tablespoons sherry. Stir in a little hot liquid, tip into pan, stir and simmer until thickened.

■ COOK'S TIP

Couscous is a pre-cooked grain, so it only needs to be soaked in water, which it will absorb, as described in the recipe, then heated through.

63 VEGETABLE LAYER

Preparation time:
20 minutes

Cooking time:
45 minutes

Oven temperature:
200 C/400 F/gas 6

Serves 4

Calories:
315 per portion

YOU WILL NEED:
1 kg/2 lb fresh spinach, washed and
    stalks removed
1 small cauliflower, cut into florets
salt and pepper
100 g/4 oz low-fat vegetarian Cheddar,
    grated
225 g/8 oz tomatoes, skinned and sliced
2 tablespoons chopped fresh parsley
100 g/4 oz button mushrooms, sliced
600 ml/1 pint natural yogurt
3 eggs
pinch of grated nutmeg
25 g/1 oz jumbo oats

Cook the spinach, without added water, over moderate heat for about 10 minutes, stirring frequently until the leaves have wilted. Turn into a colander and press it to extract the moisture. Cook the cauliflower in boiling, salted water for about 10 minutes until the florets are beginning to soften.

Place the spinach in a shallow, greased baking dish. Sprinkle with 25 g/1 oz of the cheese. Cover with the tomatoes, season with pepper, sprinkle on 1 tablespoon of the parsley, then cover with the mushrooms and the cauliflower.

In a bowl, beat the yogurt and beat in the eggs. Season with salt, pepper and nutmeg and stir in 50 g/2 oz of the cheese. Pour the sauce over the vegetables. Mix the remaining cheese and parsley with the oats and sprinkle on top.

Place the dish on a baking sheet and cook in a preheated oven for 30 minutes or until the topping is brown.

■ COOK'S TIP

Parsley is especially rich in vitamins A and C, and also iron, iodine and calcium. It is said that chewing a sprig freshens the breath, especially after eating garlic.

64 RATATOUILLE AU GRATIN

Preparation time:
30 minutes

Cooking time:
50 minutes

Oven temperature:
190 C/375 F/gas 5

Serves 4

Calories:
486 per portion

YOU WILL NEED:
6 tablespoons olive oil
1 small aubergine, sliced
2 garlic cloves, crushed
350 g/12 oz courgettes, sliced
1 red pepper, cored, seeded and sliced
350 g/12 oz tomatoes, skinned and
    sliced
1 tablespoon chopped fresh basil
salt and pepper
450 g/1 lb potatoes, boiled and sliced
225 g/8 oz Mozzarella cheese, thinly
    sliced

Heat half the oil in a frying pan, add the aubergine and fry on both sides until just beginning to brown, adding more oil if necessary. Remove from the pan and drain on kitchen paper.

Add the remaining oil to the pan and fry the garlic, courgettes and red pepper for 8-10 minutes, until softened, stirring occasionally. Add the tomatoes, basil, aubergine and salt and pepper to taste and simmer for 10 minutes.

Place the potatoes in a shallow ovenproof dish and cover with the ratatouille. Spread evenly to the edges and arrange the cheese slices over the top. Bake in a preheated moderately hot oven for 15-20 minutes, until the cheese begins to melt. Serve immediately.

■ COOK'S TIP

For a lower fat version, steam the sliced aubergines gently over simmering water for about 3 minutes instead of frying them.

65 SAVOURY SANDWICH PUDDING

Preparation time:
20 minutes

Cooking time:
45 minutes

Oven temperature:
180 C/350 F/gas 4

Serves 4

Calories:
297 per portion

YOU WILL NEED:
25 g/1 oz butter
6 slices brown bread from a small loaf, crusts removed
100 g/4 oz vegetarian Cheddar cheese, grated
3 tomatoes, skinned and sliced
2 eggs
½ teaspoon made English mustard
salt and pepper
pinch of cayenne pepper
300 ml/½ pint milk

Lightly oil a 900 ml/1½ pint pie dish.

Butter the bread and make 3 sandwiches using 75 g/3 oz of the cheese and the tomatoes. Cut each one into 4 triangles and arrange in the dish.

Whisk together the eggs, mustard, salt, pepper, cayenne pepper and milk and gently pour over the sandwiches.

Sprinkle the remaining cheese on top and place near the top of the oven for about 45 minutes until puffed and golden.

66 NUT-STUFFED MARROW

Preparation time:
20 minutes

Cooking time:
45 minutes-1 hour

Oven temperature:
180 C/350 F/gas 4

Serves 4

Calories:
270 per portion

YOU WILL NEED:
1 medium marrow
1 large onion, finely chopped
1 garlic clove, crushed
2 tablespoons olive oil
225 g/8 oz fresh spinach, cooked and drained
100 g/4 oz button mushrooms, finely chopped
50 g/2 oz chopped pine nuts
25 g/1 oz chopped toasted almonds
2 hard-boiled eggs, chopped
salt and pepper

Cut a slice from each end of the marrow, about 1 cm/½ inch thick. Slice the marrow in half horizontally and scoop out and discard all the centre seeds.

Fry the onion and garlic gently in the olive oil for 4-5 minutes; mix with the remaining ingredients, to make a firm stuffing.

Pack the stuffing tightly into the marrow halves and wrap each half securely in foil. Bake in a preheated oven for about 45 minutes-1 hour until the marrow is tender.

Serve hot, cut into thick slices, accompanied by New potatoes with fennel and mint (see recipe 94).

■ COOK'S TIP

Accompanied by a crisp green salad and followed by fresh fruit, this would make a satisfying and calcium-rich meal. Serve on its own for a light lunch.

■ COOK'S TIP

Instead of using marrow, try using peppers. Select a variety of colours and blanch in boiling water for a few minutes. Drain, plunge into cold water and drain again.

Cut a slice from the stalk end of each pepper (for 'lids'), remove core and seeds, fill with stuffing, replace 'lids' and bake as above.

67 GOUGERE WITH RATATOUILLE

Preparation time:
50 minutes

Cooking time:
about 40 minutes

Oven temperature:
220 C/425 F/gas 7

Serves 4

Calories:
262 per portion

YOU WILL NEED:
50 g/2 oz hard vegetable margarine
150 ml/5 fl oz water
salt
65 g/2 ½ oz plain wholemeal flour
2 eggs (size 3), beaten
black pepper
½ teaspoon made English mustard
50 g/2 oz mature vegetarian Cheddar
  cheese, grated
Ratatouille filling (see Cook's Tip)
1 tablespoon chopped parsley, to garnish

Make the choux pastry. Put the margarine, water and ¼ tea-spoon salt in a large pan. Have the flour ready on a small plate nearby. Bring the margarine and water to a fast boil, draw the pan off the heat and tip in the flour all at once. Beat briskly with a wooden spoon until the mixture forms a ball that rolls cleanly around the pan. Leave to cool for 5 minutes.

Slowly add the beaten egg, a little at a time, beating well between each addition. When all the egg is incorporated, beat in plenty of black pepper, the mustard and the grated cheese. Place adjoining heaped teaspoons of the mixture in a 25 cm/10 inch circle on a greased baking tray, leaving rough peaks. Bake in a preheated oven for about 40 minutes, or until the choux pastry is puffy and brown. Transfer to a heated platter and spoon in the ratatouille filling. Serve garnished with parsley.

68 VEGETABLE GRATIN

Preparation time:
20 minutes

Cooking time:
40 minutes

Oven temperature:
200 C/400 F/gas 6

Serves 4

Calories:
311 per portion

YOU WILL NEED:
750 g/1 ½ lb parsnips, peeled and sliced
1 large onion, peeled and sliced
225 g/8 oz carrots, scraped and sliced
225 g/8 oz courgettes, sliced
175 g/6 oz cauliflower florets
225 g/8 oz grated vegetarian Cheddar
  cheese
salt and pepper

Boil the parsnips and onion in 2.5 cm/1 inch water for 5-7 minutes, until nearly tender. In a separate saucepan boil or steam the carrots, courgettes and cauliflower for about 5 minutes, until nearly tender. Drain both lots of vegetables (keeping the cooking water for soup or stock).

Grease a large shallow ovenproof dish. Put half the onion mixture in a layer in the base, sprinkle with a third of the cheese, the carrots, courgettes and cauliflower. Sprinkle with another third of the cheese and a little seasoning. Cover with the remaining onion mixture and the cheese. Bake in a pre-heated oven for 30 minutes.

■ COOK'S TIP

A basic Ratatouille includes onion, aubergine, courgettes, green and red peppers and tomatoes, all coarsely chopped or diced and cooked to a thick stew with 1-2 tablespoons oil, tomato purée and seasoning to taste, and chopped fresh basil.

■ COOK'S TIP

Use a fully matured Cheddar to give this dish plenty of flavour. Try using other vegetables such as broccoli, potato, French green beans, swede or turnip.

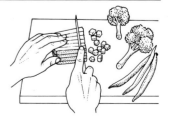

69 ROULADE WITH MUSHROOM FILLING

Preparation time:
30 minutes

Cooking time:
20 minutes

Oven temperature:
200 C/400 F/gas 6

Serves 4

Calories:
278 per portion

YOU WILL NEED:
Mushroom filling (see Cook's Tip)
5 eggs, separated (see recipe 72)
salt and pepper
½ teaspoon made English mustard
1 teaspoon vinegar
100 g/4 oz grated mature vegetarian
  Cheddar cheese
1 tablespoon grated Parmesan cheese
1 bunch watercress, chopped

Line a 23 × 33 cm/9 × 13 inch Swiss roll tin with greased greaseproof paper. Make the filling.

For the roulade, whisk the egg yolks, salt, pepper, mustard and vinegar in a small bowl until light and thick. Fold in the Cheddar. In a large bowl, whisk the egg whites until stiff. Take 2 tablespoons of the whisked whites and fold them into the cheese and yolk mixture to loosen it, then spoon it into the remaining whites and gently fold together. Pour the mixture into the prepared tin and smooth the surface. Bake near the top of a preheated oven for 10-12 minutes until risen and golden brown. Remove from the oven but leave the oven on.

Sprinkle a sheet of greaseproof paper with Parmesan cheese and turn the roulade on to it. Peel off the greaseproof lining.

Gently reheat the filling, but do not let it boil, and spoon it over the roulade. Sprinkle with watercress, then roll the roulade up. Return to the oven for about 4 minutes.

■ COOK'S TIP

Mushroom filling: fry 1 chopped shallot in a little oil. Add 225 g/8 oz chopped mushrooms. Cook 2-3 minutes. Add 65 ml/ 2½ fl oz each white wine,

vegetable stock, and seasoning. Cook gently 5 minutes, then boil rapidly to reduce liquid to 2 tablespoons. Add 3 tablespoons double cream.

70 CREAMY ONION FLAN

Preparation time:
20 minutes

Cooking time:
1 hour 20 minutes

Oven temperature:
200 C/400 F/gas 6
then
180 C/350 F/gas 4

Serves 4

Calories:
295 per portion

YOU WILL NEED:
100 g/4 oz self-raising wholewheat
  flour
¼ teaspoon salt
65 g/2½ oz butter or margarine
1 tablespoon cold water
FOR THE FILLING
450 g/1 lb onions, sliced
15 g/½ oz butter or margarine
150 ml/5 fl oz single cream
2 egg yolks
salt and pepper
grated nutmeg
chopped parsley, to garnish

Sift the flour and salt into a bowl, then add 50 g/2 oz of the fat; rub it into the flour until the mixture resembles breadcrumbs. Add the water, then press the mixture together to make a dough. Roll out on a lightly-floured board, then use to line a 20 cm/8 inch flan tin. Lightly prick the base of the flan. Bake for 15-20 minutes, until the pastry is firm and golden brown. Just before you take the flan out of the oven, put the remaining 15 g/½ oz fat into a small saucepan and melt. When the flan case is cooked, use the hot fat to brush the inside surface. Turn the oven setting down to 180 C/350 F/gas 4.

Fry the onions in the butter or margarine for 15-20 minutes, until very soft. Take off the heat and add the cream, egg yolks, salt, pepper and nutmeg. Pour into the flan case, and bake for 30-35 minutes until just set. Serve the flan sprinkled with parsley.

■ COOK'S TIP

While making the pastry, place a baking tray in the oven to heat. If you place the flan tin on the baking tray while cooking the pastry, the flan will have a crisper base.

71 COURGETTE FLAN

Preparation time: 35 minutes	YOU WILL NEED: *175 g/6 oz plain wholemeal flour*
	salt and pepper
Cooking time: 35 minutes	*75 g/3 oz hard vegetable margarine* *3 tablespoons water*
	1 tablespoon vegetable oil
Oven temperature: 200 C/400 F/gas 6	FOR THE FILLING *1 tablespoon vegetable oil*
Serves 4	*3 courgettes, about 100 g/4 oz, sliced*
	2 bunches watercress, stalks removed
Calories: 373 per portion	*2 eggs* *150 ml/5 fl oz soured cream*
	5 tablespoons milk

Make the pastry. Put the flour and ¼ teaspoon salt in a bowl and rub in the margarine until the texture resembles fine breadcrumbs. Mix to a firm dough with the water and oil. Roll out on a floured surface and use to line a 20 cm/8 inch fluted flan ring. Place the flan on a baking sheet and bake in a preheated oven for 15 minutes to set the pastry without browning.

Meanwhile, prepare the filling. Heat the oil in a pan and fry the courgettes quickly on both sides until brown. Drain. Fry the watercress for 30 seconds until soft, and chop coarsely. Spread the courgettes and watercress over the base of the flan.

Put the eggs, soured cream, milk, salt and pepper into a bowl and whisk together. Pull the centre shelf of the preheated oven out slightly and place the flan case on it, then pour the egg and cream mixture over the courgettes and slide the shelf gently into place. Bake for 25 minutes until the flan is set and lightly browned on top.

▦ COOK'S TIP

The flan can be made up to 24 hours in advance and kept covered in the refrigerator. Warm through gently in a moderate oven before serving.

72 SPINACH ROULADE

Preparation time: 30 minutes	YOU WILL NEED: *900 g/2 lb fresh spinach*
	15 g/½ oz butter or margarine
Cooking time: 35 minutes	*salt and pepper* *4 eggs, separated (see Cook's Tip)*
Oven temperature: 200 C/400 F/gas 6	*a little grated Parmesan cheese* FOR THE FILLING
	15 g/½ oz butter or margarine
Serves 4	*175 g/6 oz button mushrooms, wiped and sliced*
Calories: 376 per portion	*300 ml/½ pint soured cream* *grated nutmeg*

Cook the spinach in a saucepan without water for about 10 minutes, until the spinach is tender, drain thoroughly and chop. Add the butter or margarine, seasoning and the egg yolks.

Line a shallow 18 × 28 cm/7 × 11 inch Swiss roll tin with greased greaseproof paper to cover the base of the tin and extend 5 cm/2 inches up each side. Sprinkle with Parmesan cheese. Whisk the egg whites until stiff and fold them into the spinach mixture. Pour into the tin and bake in a preheated oven for 10-15 minutes, until risen and springy to touch.

Make the filling. Heat the fat in a saucepan and fry the mushrooms over a high heat for 2-3 minutes. Add the soured cream, a little salt, pepper and nutmeg and heat gently.

Turn the cooked roulade out on to greaseproof paper dusted with Parmesan; strip off the first greaseproof paper. Spread the filling over the roulade and roll it up. Slide on to an ovenproof dish, return to the oven and heat through for 5 minutes. Serve garnished with watercress if liked.

▦ COOK'S TIP

To separate the egg white from the yolk, crack the shell in two over a bowl. Catch the yolk in one half of the shell and let the white fall into the bowl.

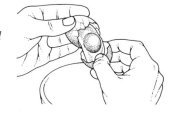

73 ASPARAGUS LOAF

Preparation time:
20 minutes

Cooking time:
1 hour

Oven temperature:
190 C/375 F/gas 5

Serves 4

Calories:
333 per portion

YOU WILL NEED:
1 small onion, grated
100 g/4 oz grated Parmesan
100 g/4 oz ground almonds
2 eggs
150 ml/¼ pint single cream
salt and pepper
freshly grated nutmeg
450 g/1 lb cooked, trimmed green
*   asparagus (make sure that all the*
*   tough part has been removed)*
sprigs of parsley or watercress, to
*   garnish*

Grease a 450 g/1 lb loaf tin and line with a long strip of greaseproof paper to cover the base and the short sides. Mix together the onion, cheese, almonds, eggs and cream. Season with salt, pepper and grated nutmeg. Put a layer of this mixture in the bottom of the loaf tin, then arrange a layer of asparagus spears on top. Continue in layers like this until all the ingredients are used up, ending with the nut mixture. Bake in a preheated oven for 45-60 minutes, until risen and firm in the centre. Cool in the tin, then slip a knife round the sides and carefully turn out on to a plate. Strip off the paper. Cut into slices, then cut in half again. Arrange the slices on a plate and garnish with parsley or watercress.

74 SWEDE AND APPLE CASSEROLE

Preparation time:
15 minutes

Cooking time:
50 minutes

Oven temperature:
180 C/350 F/gas 4

Serves 4

Calories:
180 per portion

YOU WILL NEED:
750 g/1 ½ lb swede, cubed
salt and pepper
1 large cooking apple, peeled, cored
*   and sliced*
500 g/2 oz light soft brown sugar
25 g/1 oz butter
3-4 tablespoons medium sherry
*   (optional)*

Cook the swede in boiling, salted water for 20-30 minutes or until tender. Drain well.

Put half the swede in a greased casserole and cover with half the apple slices. Sprinkle over half the brown sugar and salt and pepper to taste. Dot with half the butter. Repeat the layers. Sprinkle over the sherry, if using.

Cover and cook in a preheated oven for 30 minutes. Serve with baked potatoes or crusty French bread.

■ COOK'S TIP

It's well worth taking the time to arrange the asparagus neatly into the loaf tin. Season carefully as the Parmesan tends to be salty. This loaf also makes a lovely summer dinner party dish, served with mayonnaise, mangetout peas and some crisp lettuce.

■ COOK'S TIP

If preparing the apple in advance, remember to sprinkle over some lemon juice to prevent it going brown. Bramley apples are ideal for this dish.

75 SWEETCORN AND TOMATO BAKE

Preparation time:
20 minutes

Cooking time:
about 50 minutes

Oven temperature:
220 C/425 F/gas 7

Serves 4

Calories:
284 per portion

YOU WILL NEED:
3 tablespoons oil
1 garlic clove, peeled
275 g/9 oz tomatoes, cut into wedges
1 green pepper, cored, seeded and
 chopped
1 × 326 g/11 ½ oz can sweetcorn
salt and pepper
pinch of grated nutmeg
2 tablespoons unsalted peanuts,
 chopped
4-5 tablespoons double cream
1 egg yolk
2 egg whites

Heat the oil in a pan, add the garlic and fry until golden brown. Remove with a slotted spoon and discard. Add the tomatoes and green pepper and cook for 5 minutes. Add the sweetcorn with the can juice, salt and pepper to taste and the nutmeg. Cook, over a low heat, for about 8 minutes. Transfer to a medium ovenproof dish or a 1.2 litre/2 pint soufflé dish and stir in the peanuts.

Mix the cream with the egg yolk and stir into the vegetable mixture, blending well. Whisk the egg whites until they stand in stiff peaks, then fold into the vegetable mixture with a metal spoon. Cook in a preheated hot oven for 25-30 minutes.

76 SPANISH VEGETABLE OMELETTE

Preparation time:
30 minutes

Cooking time:
30 minutes

Serves 4-6

Calories:
446-298 per portion

YOU WILL NEED:
8 tablespoons olive oil
4 large potatoes, peeled and cubed
2 onions, chopped
1 red pepper, cored, seeded and
 chopped or cut into strips
1 green pepper, cored, seeded and
 chopped or cut into strips
2 courgettes, cut into julienne strips
2 small aubergines, finely chopped
2-3 garlic cloves, crushed or finely
 chopped
350 g/12 oz tomatoes, finely chopped
4 eggs
salt and pepper

Heat 5 tablespoons of the oil in a pan, add the potatoes and fry, over a low heat, turning frequently for about 15 minutes.

Meanwhile, heat the remaining oil in a large non-stick frying pan. Add the onions, peppers, courgettes and aubergines and fry, over a low heat, for about 8-10 minutes. Just before the vegetables are cooked, add the garlic, tomatoes and the cooked potatoes.

Beat the eggs with a little salt and black pepper. Pour the mixture evenly over the vegetables and cook, over a low heat, until the egg has just set.

Turn the omelette out on to a large plate and serve cut into wedges with a crisp salad.

■ COOK'S TIP

This savoury bake is delicious and very filling. It can be served as a meal in itself with French bread or Mangetout in garlic butter (see recipe 99).

■ COOK'S TIP

A Spanish omelette offers many possibilities for variation. The potato, onion, garlic and peppers are a must (the peppers especially, as these make the omelette juicy *and moist), but the remaining vegetables can be replaced with others of your choice. It provides an ideal opportunity to use leftovers.*

77 SOUFFLE CHEESE POTATOES

Preparation time:
25 minutes

Cooking time:
about 1½ hours

Oven temperature:
190 C/375 F/gas 5

Serves 4

Calories:
291 per portion

YOU WILL NEED:
4 medium potatoes, washed
20 g/¾ oz butter
salt and pepper
100 g/4 oz vegetarian curd cheese
2 tablespoons grated Parmesan cheese
2 teaspoons French or wholegrain mustard
2 eggs, separated (see recipe 72)

Place the potatoes on a baking sheet and bake in a preheated oven for about 1¼ hours, until tender. Cut a lengthways slice from the top of each potato; carefully scoop most of the centre potato into a bowl, leaving a shell.

Mix the scooped-out potato with the butter, salt and pepper to taste, curd cheese, 1 tablespoon of Parmesan, the mustard and egg yolks.

Whisk the egg whites until stiff but not dry; fold lightly into the potato mixture. Spoon into the potato shells then sprinkle with the remaining cheese.

Return the potatoes to the oven for a further 15-20 minutes, until well risen, golden and puffed. Serve immediately with a crisp salad.

78 BROCCOLI SOUFFLE

Preparation time:
15-20 minutes

Cooking time:
45-50 minutes

Oven temperature:
190 C/375 F/gas 5

Serves 4

Calories:
355 per portion

YOU WILL NEED:
450 g/1 lb broccoli
salt
2 tablespoons butter
2 tablespoons plain flour
150 ml/¼ pint skimmed milk
3 tablespoons dry white wine
black pepper
4 eggs, separated (see recipe 72)
3 tablespoons grated Parmesan cheese
2 tablespoons wholemeal breadcrumbs

Cook the broccoli in boiling, salted water until quite tender. Drain very thoroughly and liquidize.

Heat the butter in a pan; stir in the flour and cook for 1 minute. Gradually stir in the milk and wine; bring to the boil, stirring until the sauce has thickened.

Stir in the broccoli purée, salt and pepper to taste, egg yolks and 2 tablespoons of the Parmesan cheese.

Grease a 1.5 litre/2½ pint soufflé dish and sprinkle with the breadcrumbs. Whisk the egg whites until stiff but not dry; fold lightly into the broccoli mixture. Transfer to the prepared souf- flé dish and sprinkle with the remaining cheese.

Bake in a preheated oven for 25-30 minutes, until risen and golden. The soufflé will not rise as high as a standard soufflé. Serve immediately.

■ COOK'S TIP

Try different cheeses to vary the flavour. Choose a soft cheese with garlic and herbs, instead of curd cheese; vegetarian Stilton or Gouda instead of the Parmesan.

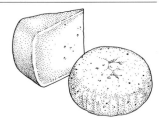

■ COOK'S TIP

Broccoli is a good source of vitamins A, B2 and C. It also supplies a good amount of iron. Choose broccoli heads which are a good colour and look fresh.

79 VEGETABLE-CHEESE SOUFFLE

Preparation time:
30 minutes

Cooking time:
40 minutes

Oven temperature:
220 C/425 F/gas 7

Serves 4

Calories:
319 per portion

YOU WILL NEED:
225 g/8 oz peeled potatoes
225 g/8 oz prepared cauliflower,
carrots, swede, parsnips or Brussels
sprouts (or a mixture)
4 tablespoons single cream
3 eggs, separated
100 g/4 oz vegetarian Cheddar cheese,
grated
salt and pepper

Cook the potatoes in boiling, salted water until tender. At the same time, cook the cauliflower or other vegetables in boiling, salted water. Drain well.

Mash the potatoes with the other vegetables until quite smooth, then beat in the cream, egg yolks, grated cheese, and salt and pepper to taste.

Whisk the egg whites until stiff, then fold into the vegetable mixture. Spoon into a greased 18 cm/7 inch soufflé dish.

Bake in a preheated oven for 20 minutes until well risen and lightly coloured on top. Serve immediately with a mixed salad.

80 CURRIED VEGEBURGERS

Preparation time:
30 minutes

Cooking time:
15 minutes

Serves 4

Calories:
175 per portion

YOU WILL NEED:
2 tablespoons oil
2 onions, chopped
1 garlic clove, crushed
2 carrots, chopped
2 celery sticks, chopped
2 teaspoons curry powder
2 tablespoons chopped parsley
450 g/1 lb potatoes, boiled and mashed
salt and pepper
fresh wholemeal breadcrumbs
oil for shallow-frying

Heat the oil in a pan, add the onions and fry until softened. Add the garlic, carrots and celery and fry for 5 minutes, stirring. Mix in the curry powder and cook for 1 minute.

Add the fried vegetables and parsley to the potato and season with salt and pepper to taste. Divide the mixture into 8 pieces, shape into rounds, and coat with breadcrumbs. Press to flatten slightly and fry for 2 minutes on each side until golden. Serve with a tomato sauce (see recipe 52).

■ COOK'S TIP

Instead of Cheddar cheese
try using something different.
Vegetarian Stilton, Edam,
Gruyère or Red Leicester are
all good alternatives which
add an individual flavour.

■ COOK'S TIP

For a filling snack, place a
vegeburger in a wholemeal
bun with some salad, a slice
of vegetarian Cheddar, and
some tomato relish.

81   LETTUCE PARCELS

Preparation time:
45 minutes, plus
chilling

Serves 4

Calories:
435 per portion

YOU WILL NEED:
8 tablespoons cooked brown rice (see
    recipe 155)
3 spring onions, finely chopped
3 hard-boiled eggs, shelled and finely
    chopped
175 g/6 oz vegetarian cottage cheese,
    sieved
1 tablespoon chopped fresh tarragon
2 tablespoons low calorie mayonnaise
16 leaves from a round lettuce
Avocado sauce (see Cook's Tip)
FOR THE GARNISH
12 mangetout, blanched
1 small red pepper, cored, seeded and
    cut into matchstick strips

Mix the cooked rice with the spring onions, hard-boiled eggs, cottage cheese, tarragon, mayonnaise and salt and pepper.

Trim the excess stalk from the lettuce leaves. Cup one lettuce leaf in your hand; place an eighth of the rice mixture in the centre, and fold the lettuce leaf over and around it. Wrap another lettuce leaf over the top, and place 'seam-side' down in a shallow serving dish, or a platter with a rim.

Repeat with the remaining lettuce leaves and rice filling, so that you have 8 parcels in all.

Spoon the prepared sauce over the lettuce parcels – if the sauce seems too thick, thin it down with extra vegetable stock. Chill for 1 hour.

Garnish with mangetout and strips of red pepper.

■ COOK'S TIP

For the sauce, peel, halve and stone an avocado; chop the flesh and put in a liquidizer with 1 clove garlic, 1 drained, canned pimento, 1 tablespoon lemon juice and the zest from ½ a lemon, 150 ml/¼ pint vegetable stock and seasoning. Blend until smooth; chill for 2 hours.

82   SPINACH SOUFFLE

Preparation time:
15 minutes

Cooking time:
1-1¼ hours

Oven temperature:
180 C/350 F/gas 4

Serves 4

Calories:
300 per portion

YOU WILL NEED:
165 g/5 ½ oz frozen or fresh leaf
    spinach, chopped
50 g/2 oz butter
½ onion, finely chopped
salt and pepper
25 g/1 oz plain flour
150 ml/¼ pint milk
3 eggs, separated
½ teaspoon dried thyme
25 g/1 oz vegetarian Cheddar cheese,
    finely grated

Grease a 15 cm/6 inch soufflé dish.

Heat the frozen or fresh spinach over a low heat and add 15 g/½ oz of the butter. Stir in the onion and season well. Leave to cook gently.

Melt the remaining butter in another pan and stir in the flour. Cook for a few minutes. Allow to cool slightly before gradually stirring in the milk. Bring to the boil, stirring, and simmer until thickened. Cook for a further 3 minutes. Allow to cool, then add the egg yolks, beating in well. Stir in the thyme and cheese.

Stir the sauce into the spinach mixture. Whisk the egg whites until just holding their shape and fold into the spinach mixture using a metal spoon. Spoon into the soufflé dish.

Bake in a preheated oven for 45-50 minutes until risen and golden brown. Serve immediately.

■ COOK'S TIP

Spinach has a very high vitamin A content and is rich in iron and vitamin C. It will keep for a short time in the fridge, but it is best eaten as soon as possible after buying.

83 LEEK AND EGG PUFFS

Preparation time:
30 minutes (or 45
minutes if making
pastry)

Cooking time:
30 minutes

Oven temperature:
220 C/425 F/gas 7

Serves 4

Calories:
351 per portion

YOU WILL NEED:
1 medium leek, about 200 g/7 oz,
   washed and sliced
salt and pepper
1 tablespoon vegetable oil
1 small onion, thinly sliced
½ teaspoon coriander seeds, crushed
50 g/2 oz mature vegetarian Cheddar
   cheese, cut into small cubes
225 g/8 oz frozen and thawed puff
   pastry
2 hard-boiled eggs, shelled and halved
   lengthways
beaten egg, for glazing

Cook the sliced leek in boiling, salted water for 6 minutes, then strain and set aside.

Heat the oil in a small pan and fry the onion until golden brown. Add salt, pepper and coriander then stir in the cooked leek. Allow the mixture to cool slightly and stir in the cheese. Roll out the pastry thinly and trim to a 30 cm/12 inch square. Cut it into four 10 cm/4 inch squares. Cut the trimmings into leaf shapes to decorate the puffs.

Brush the edges of each pastry square with beaten egg. Divide the filling between the squares, placing it just off centre, and top with half a boiled egg. Fold the pastry over to make a triangle. Seal the edges firmly and brush the tops with beaten egg. Arrange the pastry leaves on top and brush with beaten egg. Bake in a preheated oven for 15-20 minutes until puffed up and golden brown. Serve hot.

84 POTATO AND PEA CURRY

Preparation time:
20 minutes

Cooking time:
20 minutes

Serves 4

Calories:
301 per portion,
with Turmeric rice;
177 per portion,
without rice

**Suitable for vegans
using soya margarine**

YOU WILL NEED:
2 tablespoons butter or soya margarine
1 onion, chopped
2 teaspoons each turmeric, ground
   cumin and ground coriander
¼ teaspoon chilli powder
2 bay leaves
1 × 225 g/8 oz can tomatoes
450 g/1 lb potatoes, peeled and
   quartered
300 ml/½ pint water
salt and pepper
300 g/10 oz packet frozen peas

Melt the butter or soya margarine in a large saucepan and fry the onion until soft. Stir in the spices and bay leaves. Add the remaining ingredients. Bring to the boil, then cover and simmer for 15 minutes. Serve with Turmeric rice (see Cook's Tip), and Spiced okra (see recipe 111).

■ COOK'S TIP

*Try making the puffs with
the Extra light pastry in
recipe 88. The pastry is good
eaten cold, making the puffs
a good picnic or packed
lunch dish.*

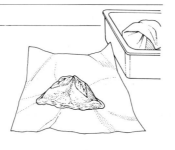

■ COOK'S TIP

*For Turmeric rice, heat
1 ½ tablespoons oil in a pan,
add 225 g/8 oz uncooked
brown rice and fry for 3-4
minutes. Stir in ¾ teaspoon
turmeric, 3 cloves and a bay*
*leaf. Cook for a few seconds,
then stir in 600 ml/1 pint
water and seasoning. Bring
to boil, then simmer for
40-45 minutes until tender.*

85 COURGETTE MOUSSAKA

Preparation time:
20 minutes

Cooking time:
50 minutes

Oven temperature:
200 C/400 F/gas 6

Serves 4

Calories:
576 per portion

YOU WILL NEED:
750 g/1 ½ lb courgettes, thinly sliced
120 ml/4 fl oz olive oil
1 large onion, thinly sliced
2 green peppers, cored, seeded and
   diced
1 garlic clove, crushed
450 g/1 lb tomatoes, skinned and sliced
1 tablespoon tomato purée
1 tablespoon chopped fresh mint
salt and pepper
100 g/4 oz Gruyère cheese, thinly sliced
2 tablespoons plain flour
300 ml/½ pint natural yogurt
2 egg yolks
75 g/3 oz vegetarian Cheddar, grated

Fry the courgette slices a few at a time in the oil over a moderate heat. Turn them to brown evenly. Set aside.

Fry the onion, peppers and garlic in the pan for about 4 minutes, stirring once or twice. Add a little more oil if necessary. Stir in the tomatoes, tomato purée, mint, and salt and pepper to taste. Cook for a further 2 minutes.

Arrange a layer of courgettes in a greased, shallow baking dish. Cover with half the tomato mixture, then with the sliced cheese. Make a layer of the remaining tomato mixture, and cover with the remaining courgette slices.

Mix together the flour, yogurt, egg yolks, grated cheese, and salt and pepper to taste. Pour over the courgettes. Cook in a preheated oven for 25 minutes, until the top is golden brown.

■ COOK'S TIP

Courgettes are baby marrows which are also known as zucchini in America. Choose smooth, brightly coloured and firm courgettes. Keep them in a cool place.

86 CHEESE CRUST PIE

Preparation time:
1 hour

Cooking time:
45 minutes

Oven temperature:
200 C/400 F/gas 6,
then
180 C/350 F/gas 4

Serves 4

Calories:
622 per portion

YOU WILL NEED:
FOR THE CHEESE PASTRY
175 g/6 oz plain flour
pinch of salt
100 g/4 oz butter, cubed
75 g/3 oz vegetarian Cheddar cheese,
   finely grated
2-3 tablespoons cold water, to mix
1 egg, beaten, to glaze
FOR THE FILLING
50 g/2 oz butter
1 onion, sliced
3 carrots, sliced
1 × 200 g/7 oz can sweetcorn kernels
50 g/2 oz mushrooms, sliced
2 celery sticks, chopped
1 × 50 g/2 oz packet leek soup

For the pastry, sift the flour and salt into a mixing bowl. Rub in the butter and stir in the cheese. Bind with water. Wrap and chill until needed.

For the filling, melt the butter in a pan and fry the vegetables for a few minutes. Drain. Make up the packet of leek soup as directed, but using 600 ml/1 pint water only. Stir in the vegetables and pour into a 750 ml/1½ pint pie dish.

Roll out the pastry to top the pie, trim and flute the edges. Use the pastry trimmings to make leaves for the top. Brush the pastry with egg and bake in a preheated oven for 15 minutes; reduce the heat and bake for a further 20 minutes. Serve hot.

■ COOK'S TIP

For pastry packed with protein, add 50 g/2 oz ground walnuts or hazelnuts instead of 50 g/2 oz of the flour. It will add a delicious rich, nutty flavour to the pie.

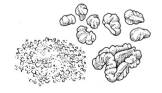

87 INDIVIDUAL ASPARAGUS FLANS

Preparation time:
20 minutes

Cooking time:
35 minutes

Oven temperature:
200 C/400 F/gas 6,
then
190 C/375 F/gas 5

Serves 6

Calories:
560 per portion

YOU WILL NEED:
FOR THE PASTRY
350 g/12 oz plain wholewheat flour
½ teaspoon salt
200 g/7 oz butter or margarine
4-5 tablespoons cold water
FOR THE FILLING
1 bunch asparagus, trimmed and
  cooked (see Cook's Tip)
300 ml/½ pint single cream
2 egg yolks
salt and pepper
freshly grated nutmeg

Sift the flour and salt into a bowl, add 175 g/6 oz of the butter or margarine, then rub it into the flour with your fingertips. Add the water, and bind to a dough. Roll the dough out on a lightly-floured board, then use to line six 10 cm/4 inch flan tins. Prick the flan bases and place in a preheated oven on a baking tray. Bake for 15-20 minutes, until golden brown. Melt the remaining butter in a pan. Remove the flan cases from the oven and brush with the butter. Turn the oven down.

Trim the asparagus spears and divide between the flans. Whisk the cream and egg yolks together; season with salt, pepper and nutmeg. Pour a little of this mixture into each flan, on top of the asparagus. Return the flans to the oven and bake for about 15 minutes, until the filling has set. They should be just firm to the touch and no more.

■ COOK'S TIP

These flans make a superb summer starter. To cook asparagus, drop into a pan of boiling salted water and cook until just tender – about 3-4 minutes.

88 FAMILY VEGETABLE PIE

Preparation time:
45 minutes, plus
chilling

Cooking time:
35 minutes

Oven temperature:
200 C/400 F/gas 6

Serves 4

Calories:
572 per portion

YOU WILL NEED:
Extra light pastry (see Cook's Tip)
300 ml/½ pint salted water
100 g/4 oz carrots, sliced
100 g/4 oz leeks, sliced
100 g/4 oz celery, sliced
100 g/4 oz cauliflower, cut into florets
about 300 ml/½ pint milk
25 g/1 oz butter
25 g/1 oz plain flour
black pepper
2 tablespoons chopped fresh parsley
1 × 225 g/8 oz can red kidney beans
beaten egg, for brushing

Make the pastry. For the filling, boil the water in a pan. Put in the carrots, simmer 5 minutes, then add the remaining vegetables and cook 10 minutes.

Strain the vegetables, reserving the liquid. Make up to a generous 600 ml/1 pint with milk. Melt the butter in the pan, add the flour and cook, stirring, for 3 minutes. Pour in the milk mixture and bring to the boil, stirring, and simmer 1 minute. Add salt and pepper then the vegetables, parsley and drained beans. Pour into a 1.2 litre/2 pint pie dish with a pie funnel.

Roll out the pastry 2.5 cm/1 inch larger than the pie dish. Cut a strip off to cover the rim of the dish, brush with egg and place the lid in position. Trim and flute the edges. Cut any leftover pastry into decorations. Brush with beaten egg, arrange the decorations on the pie and brush again with egg. Bake in a preheated oven for 25 minutes until the pastry is golden brown.

■ COOK'S TIP

For the pastry: mix 175 g/ 6 oz wholemeal self-raising flour, salt and 1 teaspoon dried mixed herbs in a bowl. Mix in 100 g/4 oz grated hard vegetable margarine.

Mix gently to a dough with 3 tablespoons water and 1 tablespoon oil. Chill.

89 LITTLE LEEK QUICHES

Preparation time:
45 minutes, plus
chilling

Cooking time:
50 minutes

Oven temperature:
180 C/350 F/gas 4

Makes 8

Calories:
735 per quiche

YOU WILL NEED:
FOR THE PASTRY
450 g/1 lb plain flour
pinch of salt
350 g/12 oz butter, cubed
2 egg yolks
3 tablespoons water
FOR THE FILLING
50 g/2 oz butter
5 large leeks, sliced
1 teaspoon dried oregano
5 eggs
300 ml/½ pint single cream
salt and pepper
1 tablespoon chopped fresh parsley

For the pastry, sift the flour and salt into a mixing bowl. Rub in the butter. Bind with the egg yolks and water, then wrap and chill for 20 minutes.

Roll out the pastry dough and use to line eight 11.5 cm/4½ inch flan rings placed on baking sheets. Line the pastry cases with greaseproof paper and weigh down with baking beans. Bake in a preheated oven for 15 minutes, then remove the paper and beans and bake for a further 5 minutes.

For the filling, melt the butter in a frying pan, add the leeks and fry gently until softened. Remove from the heat and allow to cool. Sprinkle over the oregano and divide between the pastry shells. Beat together the eggs, cream and salt and pepper to taste and pour over the leeks. Sprinkle with the chopped parsley. Bake in a preheated oven for 20 minutes.

■ COOK'S TIP

The leek is a member of the onion family. If young, leeks can be chopped finely and used raw in salads. The tougher greentops are best used in long-cook hotpots.

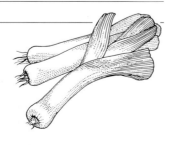

90 QUICK PIZZA

Preparation time:
30 minutes

Cooking time:
30 minutes

Oven temperature:
220 C/425 F/gas 7

Serves 4

Calories:
475 per portion

YOU WILL NEED:
225 g/8 oz self-raising wholewheat
    flour
2 teaspoons baking powder
½ teaspoon salt
50 g/2 oz butter or margarine
8-9 tablespoons water
FOR THE TOPPING
2 onions, chopped
2 tablespoons oil
2 tablespoons tomato purée
1-2 teaspoons dried oregano
salt, sugar and pepper
100 g/4 oz button mushrooms, sliced
small green pepper, seeded, chopped
    and fried
75 g/3 oz grated vegetarian Gouda
    cheese

Brush a 30 cm/12 inch round pizza plate with oil. Sift the flour and baking powder into a bowl, tipping in the residue of bran. Add the salt, rub the fat into the flour, then pour in the water and mix to a pliable dough. Roll out to fit the pizza plate. Put the dough on the plate, prick all over. Bake in a preheated oven for 10 minutes.

Meanwhile, prepare the topping. Fry the onion in the oil for 10 minutes, then remove from the heat and add the tomato purée, herbs, salt, sugar and pepper to taste. Spread the mixture on the pizza base, top with the mushrooms, and green pepper and sprinkle with cheese. Bake for 15-20 minutes.

■ COOK'S TIP

There are many different vegetables that can be used as a topping. Try broccoli, asparagus, sweetcorn, peas, or red pepper. Try Mozzarella cheese instead of *Gouda. Radish slices and parsley sprigs make a pretty garnish.*

91 SPINACH FILO PIE

Preparation time:
30-35 minutes

Cooking time:
50-55 minutes

Oven temperature:
190 C/375 F/gas 5

Serves 6

Calories:
664 per portion

YOU WILL NEED:
1 large onion, thinly sliced
8 spring onions, chopped or thinly
    sliced
6 tablespoons olive oil
100 g/4 oz butter, melted
1.25 kg/2 ½ lb fresh spinach, washed
    and shredded
salt and pepper
6 tablespoons chopped fresh parsley
4 teaspoons dried dill or oregano
3 eggs, beaten
450 g/1 lb filo pastry, thawed if frozen

Fry the onions in 4 tablespoons of the oil and 25 g/1 oz of the butter until softened. Stir in the spinach, cover and cook gently for 3-4 minutes. Drain off any excess moisture from the spinach. Season, mix in the parsley, herb and eggs.

Mix the remaining oil and butter together and use a little to grease a rectangular tin, 35 × 25 × 7.5 cm/14 × 10 × 3 inches deep. Brush a sheet of pastry with the butter and oil, and press it into the tin. Add 6 more sheets, each brushed with butter and oil. Spread the spinach filling evenly over the layers of pastry. Lay another 7 layers of oiled pastry on top. Do not press the layers down.

Brush the top layer well with butter and oil. Using a sharp knife mark squares or diamond shapes. Cut through only the top layers of pastry and not through to the spinach filling. Bake in a preheated oven for 40 minutes until golden.

92 MUSHROOM AND ONION QUICHE

Preparation time:
15 minutes

Cooking time:
about 25 minutes

Oven temperature:
200 C/400 F/gas 6

Serves 4

Calories:
408 per portion

YOU WILL NEED:
FOR THE PASTRY
225 g/8 oz plain flour
pinch salt
100 g/4 oz butter
2-3 tablespoons cold water
FOR THE FILLING
15 g/ ½ oz butter
1 large onion, thinly sliced
150 ml/ ¼ pint milk or single cream
2 eggs
salt and pepper
100 g/4 oz button mushrooms
50 g/2 oz vegetarian Cheddar, grated

Sift the flour and salt into a bowl, then rub in the butter until it resembles fine breadcrumbs. Add enough water to make a firm dough and gently knead together. Roll out the pastry and line a 20 cm/8 inch flan ring on a baking sheet or a flan dish.

For the filling, melt the butter in a frying pan, add the onion and cook gently until soft but not brown. Cool slightly and place in the pastry case.

Lightly beat together the milk, eggs and salt and pepper to taste. Reserve 3 mushrooms and finely chop the rest. Add to the egg mixture and pour into the pastry case. Thinly slice the reserved mushrooms and scatter on top. Sprinkle with the cheese. Bake in a preheated oven for 25 minutes until the pastry is cooked and the filling set.

■ COOK'S TIP

Filo pastry is available either chilled or frozen. Defrost thoroughly before use and keep the pile of pastry sheets covered with a damp teatowel while using.

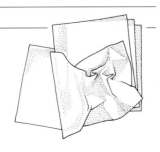

■ COOK'S TIP

Instead of using mushrooms, try a variety of other vegetables. Small broccoli florets, thinly sliced courgettes or fresh peas would work well.

VEGETABLE DISHES

Add an unusual twist to vegetables by using a variety of herbs such as mint and fennel with them. Alternatively, add nuts for a delicious, protein-rich dish. Serve with a filling main course bake or casserole for a well-balanced, nutritious meal. Select a few dishes and serve with French bread as a light supper dish.

93 BUTTON MUSHROOMS WITH GREEN PEPPERCORNS

Preparation time:
10 minutes

Cooking time:
15 minutes

Serves 4

Calories:
217 per portion

YOU WILL NEED:
450 g/1 lb small white button
   mushrooms
1 tablespoon olive oil
4 tablespoons water
salt
4 slices brown bread
2 tablespoons vegetable oil
25 g/1 oz butter
3 teaspoons green peppercorns, crushed
2 tablespoons double or whipping
   cream
coriander leaves, to garnish

Wash the mushrooms and pat them dry on kitchen paper. If they are all small leave them whole, but halve any larger ones.

Heat the oil in a large frying pan and fry the mushrooms quickly for about 5 minutes until just beginning to brown. Add the water and a little salt, cover and simmer for 10 minutes, by which time there will be a fair amount of liquid in the pan.

While the mushrooms are cooking, make the croûtons. Cut the crusts off the bread and cut the slices into 1 cm/½ inch dice. Heat the oil and butter in a frying pan until sizzling and add the bread cubes. Fry quickly until golden brown then drain on kitchen paper.

Stir the peppercorns and cream into the mushrooms and reheat gently without boiling. Tip into a warm serving dish and scatter with the croûtons. Garnish with the coriander leaves.

94 NEW POTATOES WITH FENNEL AND MINT

Preparation time:
10 minutes

Cooking time:
15-20 minutes

Serves 4

Calories:
213 per portion

**Suitable for vegans
using soya margarine**

YOU WILL NEED:
salt
1 kg/2 lb tiny new potatoes
15 g/½ oz butter or soya margarine
1 small fennel bulb, trimmed and finely
   chopped
black pepper
2 tablespoons chopped fresh mint, plus
   sprigs of mint to garnish

Bring a pan of salted water to the boil and add the potatoes. Simmer for about 15 minutes until tender and drain.

Put the butter or soya margarine into the warm pan and heat gently. Add the fennel and fry for about 5 minutes until just beginning to brown then season well with pepper.

Tip the cooked potatoes into the pan, add the mint and toss the potatoes so that they are coated with butter or soya margarine, mint and fennel.

Serve hot, garnished with sprigs of mint.

■ COOK'S TIP

A simple but unusual way to serve button mushrooms which also makes a delicious starter. Green peppercorns are sold either in jars or small cans in most *delicatessens or large stores. They are quite soft, and so can be crushed easily.*

■ COOK'S TIP

Jersey or English new potatoes are the best for this dish. When out of season or for a quick cooking dish, use canned new potatoes. Cook as instructed on the can.

95 PAN-BRAISED PEPPERS WITH TOMATO

Preparation time:
25 minutes

Cooking time:
28 minutes

Serves 4

Calories:
68 per portion

Suitable for vegans

YOU WILL NEED:
1 tablespoon vegetable oil
2 medium onions, coarsely chopped
3 large peppers, red, green and yellow, total weight about 450 g/1 lb, seeded and cut into strips
450 g/1 lb tomatoes, skinned and chopped
1 teaspoon coriander seed
1 teaspoon black peppercorns
½ teaspoon salt
½ teaspoon ground chilli

Heat the oil in a large frying pan and fry the onions for about 5 minutes until golden. Add the peppers and cook gently for 2-3 minutes, then stir in the tomatoes.

Crush the coriander seeds and peppercorns. Use a pestle and mortar if you have one; otherwise put the seeds and peppercorns between double sheets of kitchen paper and crush with a rolling pin. Add the salt and chilli to the crushed seeds and sprinkle the mixture over the peppers and tomatoes. Mix together lightly, cover the pan and cook gently for 20 minutes. This can be prepared up to 24 hours in advance and kept covered in the refrigerator.

96 FENNEL WITH WALNUTS

Preparation time:
10 minutes

Cooking time:
1 minute

Serves 4

Calories:
293 per portion

Suitable for vegans

YOU WILL NEED:
2 small fennel bulbs with leaves
FOR THE DRESSING
4 tablespoons olive oil
1 garlic clove, crushed (optional)
100 g/4 oz walnuts, chopped
salt and pepper

Slice the fennel into thin, short strips, reserving the feathery leaves. Divide between 4 individual dishes.

Heat the olive oil in a small pan and add the garlic, if using, and walnuts. Fry quickly until the walnuts just begin to brown. Add salt and pepper then spoon the hot dressing over the cold fennel strips.

Garnish the dish with the reserved fennel leaves and serve immediately.

■ COOK'S TIP

A vegetable recipe full of flavour and colour. It is not essential to use different coloured peppers, but it does look attractive. This dish is wonderful hot and almost as good served cold with a salad selection.

■ COOK'S TIP

Crisp aniseed-flavoured fennel smothered in hot walnut dressing is quick to prepare and delicious. You could also use celery instead of fennel.

97 SUMMER VEGETABLES WITH YOGURT AND MINT

Preparation time:
25 minutes

Cooking time:
15 minutes

Serves 4

Calories:
101 per portion

YOU WILL NEED:
225 g/8 oz broad beans (weighed without pods)
salt
225 g/8 oz runner beans, strings removed and sliced
225 g/8 oz peas (weighed without pods)
150 ml/5 fl oz natural yogurt
black pepper
1 tablespoon chopped fresh mint

Cook the broad beans for 8 minutes in a little boiling, salted water then drain.

Cook the runner beans and peas together for 5 minutes and drain thoroughly.

Heat the yogurt gently in one of the vegetable pans, add the vegetables and toss to coat thoroughly. Gently stir in black pepper and the mint and serve.

98 CAULIFLOWER WITH PEANUT SAUCE

Preparation time:
25 minutes

Cooking time:
15 minutes

Serves 4

Calories:
220 per portion

YOU WILL NEED:
1 cauliflower, about 500 g/1 ¼ lb
salt
2 tablespoons chopped salted peanuts, to garnish
FOR THE SAUCE
15 g/½ oz butter
15 g/½ oz plain flour
150 ml/¼ pint milk
150 ml/¼ pint vegetable stock (see recipe 3)
4 tablespoons crunchy peanut butter
½ teaspoon yeast extract
black pepper

Cut the cauliflower into florets, leaving some of the contrasting green leaves on. Cook the cauliflower in boiling salted water for about 6-8 minutes; it should be slightly crisp. Drain and keep warm in a serving dish.

While the cauliflower is cooking, make the sauce. Melt the butter in a small pan, add the flour and cook for 3 minutes, stirring all the time. Pour in the milk and vegetable stock and bring to the boil, still stirring. Simmer for 2-3 minutes then stir in the peanut butter, a spoonful at a time. The peanut butter will thicken the sauce. Add the yeast extract, a little salt if necessary and black pepper.

Pour the sauce over the cauliflower and sprinkle with the chopped peanuts. Serve hot.

■ COOK'S TIP

Frozen vegetables can be used instead, but cook for slightly less time than indicated on the packs. Use Greek yogurt for a creamier taste.

■ COOK'S TIP

If you have a grinder, try making your own peanut butter. Grind 100 g/4 oz roasted peanuts finely and mash them to a paste in a bowl, adding a little vegetable oil, if necessary. Try using hazelnuts, cashews or walnuts to vary the taste.

99 MANGETOUT IN GARLIC BUTTER

Preparation time:
15 minutes

Cooking time:
10 minutes

Serves 4

Calories:
115 per portion

**Suitable for vegans
using soya margarine**

YOU WILL NEED:
750 g/1 ½ lb mangetout, topped and
    tailed
pinch of salt
1 tablespoon oil
25 g/1 oz butter or soya margarine (see
    recipe 110)
1 garlic clove, chopped
1 tablespoon chopped parsley, to
    garnish

Place the mangetout in a pan with just enough water to cover. Add the salt and the oil. Bring to the boil, then lower the heat and cook gently for about 5-10 minutes, depending on the ripeness and freshness of the mangetout (very young pods will need only about 2 minutes).

Meanwhile, melt the butter or soya margarine in a pan, add the garlic and fry for 2 minutes. Drain the mangetout thoroughly and place in a warmed serving dish. Pour over the hot garlic butter. Sprinkle with parsley before serving.

100 KARTOSHKI

Preparation time:
5 minutes

Cooking time:
30 minutes

Serves 2-3

Calories:
315-210 per portion

**Suitable for vegans
using soya margarine**

YOU WILL NEED:
15 g/½ oz butter or soya margarine
1 tablespoon oil
450 g/1 lb small potatoes, unpeeled and
    fairly thickly sliced
salt and pepper
2 spring onions, chopped

Use the largest frying pan you have and heat the butter and oil until sizzling. Add the potatoes and stir until all the slices are coated and glistening. Keep the heat high and fry them quickly until golden brown but not cooked.

Turn the slices and sprinkle generously with salt and black pepper. Cover the frying pan, lower the heat and continue to fry/steam the slices for about 20 minutes until tender, shaking the pan occasionally to prevent them sticking. Take the lid off the pan and turn up the heat again for a minute or two.

Serve immediately sprinkled with the spring onions.

■ COOK'S TIP

*Mangetout in garlic butter is
a delicious vegetable dish to
serve with eggs. Instead of
mangetout, try using French
green beans or sliced
courgettes.*

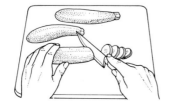

■ COOK'S TIP

*This is an economical way of
cooking potatoes, and
produces an almost roast
taste without using the oven.
It is a traditional Russian
recipe.*

101 BABY PARSNIPS IN BREADCRUMBS

Preparation time:
15 minutes

Cooking time:
30-35 minutes

Oven temperature:
220 C/425 F/gas 7

Serves 4

Calories:
118 per portion

YOU WILL NEED:
*450 g/1 lb very small parsnips,
    scrubbed if necessary*
salt
1 tablespoon vegetable oil
black pepper
75 g/3 oz fresh wholemeal breadcrumbs
*2 tablespoons freshly grated Parmesan
    cheese*
*1 tablespoon chopped fresh parsley, to
    garnish*

Cook the parsnips in boiling, salted water for 7-10 minutes until just tender. Drain and return to the pan. Toss them in the oil and plenty of black pepper.

Mix the breadcrumbs, Parmesan cheese and ½ teaspoon salt, add to the pan and toss again.

Spoon the parsnips and any crumbs left in the pan into a lightly oiled ovenproof dish and bake near the top of a pre-heated oven for 15-20 minutes until the breadcrumbs are crisp and lightly browned.

Sprinkle with chopped parsley and serve immediately.

102 BROAD BEANS WITH SESAME

Preparation time:
5 minutes for frozen beans
15 minutes for fresh beans

Cooking time:
10-15 minutes

Serves 4

Calories:
216 per portion

**Suitable for vegans
using soya margarine**

YOU WILL NEED:
*450 g/1 lb broad beans, prepared
    weight, fresh or frozen*
2 tablespoons sesame seeds
*25 g/1 oz butter or soya margarine (see
    recipe 110)*
1 tablespoon lemon juice
black pepper

Cook the beans in boiling, salted water until tender, 8-15 minutes depending on whether fresh or frozen.

While the beans are cooking, toast the sesame seeds under a moderate grill to brown them evenly.

Drain the beans, and put the butter or soya margarine in the pan. Melt it quickly and, when just beginning to brown, add the lemon juice and pepper. Tip the beans back into the pan and toss well in the butter.

Serve the beans hot, sprinkled with the sesame seeds.

▓ COOK'S TIP

If the parsnips are small, cook them whole. For larger ones, cut them in half lengthways first. Avoid really large parsnips for this recipe.

▓ COOK'S TIP

Toasted sesame seeds add a special flavour of their own to all types of vegetable dishes and seem to go particularly well with broad beans. They are a good *source of calcium, so are particularly valuable to those who do not eat dairy products.*

103 CORN ON THE COB WITH HERBS

Preparation time:
15 minutes

Cooking time:
35 minutes

Oven temperature:
200 C/400 F/gas 6

Serves 4

Calories:
221 per portion

Suitable for vegans using soya margarine

YOU WILL NEED:
4 corn cobs, husks and silky threads removed
50 g/2 oz butter or soya margarine
salt and pepper
2 teaspoons chopped mixed fresh herbs (parsley, thyme and chives)

Bring a large pan of unsalted water to the boil, add the cobs, cook for 15 minutes and drain.

Blend together the butter or soya margarine, salt, pepper and herbs. Spread a little over each corn-cob and wrap each one in a piece of baking foil, crimping the edges securely together.

Place on a baking sheet in a preheated oven for 20 minutes. Unwrap the foil parcels carefully and serve the corn on hot plates with the herb and butter juices poured over.

104 RED CABBAGE WITH APPLE

Preparation time:
15 minutes

Cooking time:
1¼-1¾ hours

Serves 4-6

Calories:
103-69 per portion

Suitable for vegans

YOU WILL NEED:
1 kg/2 lb red cabbage, shredded
2 tablespoons oil
1 onion, thinly sliced
2 cooking apples, peeled, cored and chopped
3 tablespoons wine vinegar
3 tablespoons water
1 tablespoon soft brown sugar
salt and pepper
1 tablespoon chopped parsley, to garnish

Add the cabbage to a large pan of boiling water and blanch for 2-3 minutes. Drain thoroughly. Heat the oil in a saucepan, add the onion and cook until softened, about 5 minutes. Add the apple, cover and cook for a further 5 minutes, stirring occasionally. Add the cabbage, vinegar, water, sugar, and salt and pepper to taste, blending well.

Transfer to a casserole dish. Cover and cook in a preheated moderate oven for 1-1½ hours until tender. Stir occasionally, adding a little more water if necessary. Turn into a warmed serving dish and sprinkle with parsley to serve.

■ COOK'S TIP

Use frozen corn-on-the-cob when fresh corn is out of season, but it will require 10 minutes extra boiling. It is important not to salt the cooking water for this *vegetable as it tends to make the corn kernels tough.*

■ COOK'S TIP

To shred cabbage finely, choose a long-bladed, sharp knife. Quarter the cabbage and secure each piece with your fingers, moving them back as you shred.

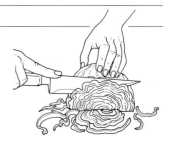

105 CELERIAC AND CARROT REMOULADE

Preparation time:
20 minutes, plus cooling

Cooking time:
10 minutes

Serves 4

Calories:
165 per portion

YOU WILL NEED:
1 celeriac root, about 225 g/8 oz, sliced into matchstick strips
225 g/8 oz carrots, sliced into matchstick strips
1 tablespoon lemon juice
salt
FOR THE DRESSING
4 tablespoons mayonnaise
150 ml/¼ pint plain Greek yogurt
1 garlic clove, crushed
1 tablespoon chopped fresh parsley
1 tablespoon finely snipped fresh chives
½ teaspoon mustard powder
pinch of cayenne pepper
1 hard-boiled egg, finely chopped
FOR THE GARNISH
1 hard-boiled egg, separated
snipped fresh chives
carrot curls (see Cook's Tip)

Partly cook the celeriac and carrot strips for 5-8 minutes in boiling, salted water with the lemon juice. Drain, dry and cool.

Mix together the dressing ingredients. Toss the celeriac and carrots in the dressing and spoon the salad on to a serving dish. Sieve the egg yolk and arrange it in the centre of the salad. Chop the white finely and place it on top, then arrange the chives around the edge and garnish with carrot curls.

◾ COOK'S TIP

For carrot curls, peel the carrots and, using a potato peeler, pare thin strips from the length of each one. Roll up the strips, secure with cocktail sticks and place in
ice-cold water for 1 hour. Drain and remove the sticks. Unroll 3 carrot curls and place them one on top of the other in opposite directions.

106 GINGERED BRUSSELS SPROUTS

Preparation time:
10 minutes, plus standing

Cooking time:
8-10 minutes

Serves 4

Calories:
79 per portion

Suitable for vegans

YOU WILL NEED:
1 ¼ kg/2 ¾ lb Brussels sprouts (see Cook's Tip)
2 tablespoons lemon juice
1 teaspoon finely grated fresh ginger or ½ teaspoon ground ginger
3-4 strips lemon rind

Steam the Brussels sprouts for 8 minutes then pour the water out of the pan under the steamer and put the sprouts into the hot pan to dry out slightly.

Sprinkle the lemon juice and ginger over, toss well and add the strips of lemon rind.

Cover and leave to stand in a warm place for 5 minutes before serving.

◾ COOK'S TIP

Prepare the sprouts by trimming the ends and removing any discoloured outer leaves. Do not cut a cross in the ends if you want them to be slightly crunchy.

107 TOFU WITH BAMBOO SHOOTS AND CARROTS

Preparation time:
15 minutes

Cooking time:
10 minutes

Serves 4

Calories:
109 per portion

Suitable for vegans

YOU WILL NEED:
2 tablespoons olive oil
225 g/8 oz firm tofu (beancurd), diced
1 teaspoon grated fresh ginger
225 g/8 oz grated carrot
225 g/8 oz can bamboo shoots, drained
1 tablespoon soy sauce
½ teaspoon sugar

Heat the olive oil in a frying pan, add the tofu and fry, turning the pieces so that they become crisp and golden on all sides. Add the remaining ingredients and stir-fry for about 2 minutes.

108 BRUSSELS SPROUTS WITH CHESTNUTS

Preparation time:
30 minutes

Cooking time:
40 minutes

Serves 4

Calories:
228 per portion

Suitable for vegans using soya margarine

YOU WILL NEED:
350 g/12 oz skinned chestnuts
25 g/1 oz butter or soya margarine (see recipe 110)
150 ml/¼ pint vegetable stock (see recipe 3)
450 g/1 lb Brussels sprouts, trimmed
salt and pepper

Slit the chestnuts with a sharp knife. Place in a pan of cold water, bring to the boil and simmer for 3 minutes. Remove the chestnuts, one at a time, and peel off their outer and inner skins.

Heat the butter or soya margarine in a small pan, add the chestnuts and cook for 5 minutes, stirring occasionally. Add the vegetable stock, bring to the boil, cover and simmer for 20 minutes.

Add the Brussels sprouts, adding more liquid if necessary, to just cover the vegetables. Add salt and pepper to taste and cook for a further 10 minutes until the sprouts are just tender. Drain the sprouts and chestnuts, reserving the stock for a soup.

▪ COOK'S TIP

Tofu, or beancurd, is made from soya beans. It is packed with protein, low in fat and simple to use. It is available in plain, marinated or smoked varieties.

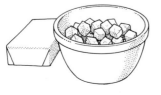

▪ COOK'S TIP

Preparing fresh chestnuts can be extremely time consuming. Use pre-cooked chestnuts in jars or cans, or dried which simply need soaking. Both are available from supermarkets and health food shops.

109 SKEWERED PEPPERS

Preparation time:
15 minutes

Cooking time:
7-10 minutes

Serves 4

Calories:
299 per portion

Suitable for vegans

YOU WILL NEED:

2 green peppers, cored, seeded and cut
    into 2.5 cm/1 inch squares
2 medium red peppers, cored, seeded
    and cut into 2.5 cm/1 inch squares
2 medium yellow peppers, cored,
    seeded and cut into 2.5 cm/1 inch
    squares
about 120 ml/4 fl oz olive oil
2 garlic cloves, finely chopped
salt
1 tablespoon crushed black peppercorns
3 tablespoons lemon juice

Thread the peppers on to 8 soaked bamboo skewers. A medium pepper will normally give about 12-16 pieces so there should be about 3-4 pieces of each colour pepper on each skewer. Alternate the colours.

Brush the peppers generously on all sides with the oil and cook under a preheated grill for 7-10 minutes, turning and basting with oil every 1-2 minutes. When they are just beginning to char they are done. Baste again with olive oil.

Put the skewers on serving plates, then sprinkle each one with a little of the finely chopped garlic, generously season with salt and pepper, then pour over some lemon juice. Serve immediately.

110 GRILLED COURGETTES WITH MUSTARD

Preparation time:
10 minutes

Cooking time:
10 minutes

Serves 4

Calories:
84 per portion

**Suitable for vegans
using soya margarine**

YOU WILL NEED:

450 g/1 lb courgettes, cut in half
    lengthways
25 g/1 oz butter or soya margarine (see
    Cook's Tip), melted
1 tablespoon Meaux mustard

Brush the courgettes with the melted butter and place them, cut side down, on a heated grill pan. Grill under high heat until lightly brown.

Turn them over and spread with the mustard. Grill until golden. Serve.

■ COOK'S TIP

In summer, cook these kebabs over a barbecue. Other vegetables can be used including mushrooms, chunks of corn on the cob and baby onions.

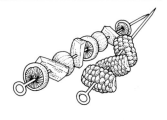

■ COOK'S TIP

Soya margarine can be used instead of butter or vegetable margarine for all dishes. It is suitable for vegans and is very low in saturated fats.

111 SPICED OKRA

Preparation time:
20 minutes

Cooking time:
30 minutes

Serves 4

Calories:
87 per portion

Suitable for vegans

YOU WILL NEED:
1 onion, chopped
2 tablespoons oil
1 garlic clove, crushed
1 teaspoon ground cumin
1 teaspoon ground coriander
2 tomatoes, skinned and chopped
1 × 225 g/8 oz can tomatoes
225 g/8 oz okra, washed and trimmed
4 tablespoons water
1 tablespoon tomato purée
salt and pepper
sugar

Fry the onion in the oil for 5 minutes without browning, then add the garlic, cumin and coriander. Stir for a couple of minutes, then add the tomatoes and okra. Add the water and tomato purée. Put a lid on the pan and leave to cook for 20 minutes, until the okra is tender, stirring from time to time. Season with salt, a pinch of sugar, and a twist or two of freshly ground black pepper.

112 SCALLOPED POTATOES

Preparation time:
20 minutes

Cooking time:
about 2 hours

Oven temperature:
180 C/350 F/gas 4

Serves 6

Calories:
162 per portion

YOU WILL NEED:
1 kg/2 lb potatoes, peeled and thinly sliced
1 large onion, thinly sliced
salt and pepper
150 ml/¼ pint vegetable stock (see recipe 3)
25 g/1 oz butter, melted

Make layers of the potatoes and onions in a well-buttered ovenproof dish, seasoning the layers with salt and pepper.

Bring the stock to the boil and pour over the potatoes, then brush liberally with the melted butter.

Cover with foil and cook in a preheated oven for 1½ hours. Remove the foil and cook for a further 30 minutes or until the potatoes are cooked through and lightly browned.

Place under a moderate grill until the potatoes are well browned and crispy on top. Serve hot.

■ COOK'S TIP

Avoid tired-looking okra or any over 10 cm/4 inches long, which are likely to be tough. Keep in the fridge and do not store longer than a couple of days.

■ COOK'S TIP

For a richer dish, use full fat milk or single cream instead of the vegetable stock. Sprinkle over 50 g/2 oz vegetarian Cheddar cheese and grill until melted.

113 PARSNIP CROQUETTES

Preparation time:
45 minutes, plus
chilling

Cooking time:
about 35 minutes

Serves 4

Calories:
421 per portion

YOU WILL NEED:

450 g/1 lb parsnips, cut into chunks
2 medium potatoes, peeled and halved
salt and pepper
50 g/2 oz plain flour, plus extra for
  coating
25 g/1 oz butter, softened
1 large egg, beaten
75 g/3 oz dried breadcrumbs
25 g/1 oz blanched almonds, chopped
vegetable oil, for deep frying
parsley sprigs, to garnish

Cook the parsnips and potatoes in boiling, salted water for about 20 minutes until tender. Drain thoroughly, then return to the rinsed-out pan and place over a gentle heat to remove excess moisture. Stir constantly to prevent the vegetables catching on the bottom of the pan. Transfer the vegetables to a bowl and leave to cool slightly, then mash until smooth.

Beat in the flour, butter and salt and pepper to taste until evenly mixed. With well-floured hands, form into 8 croquette shapes. Coat with flour, dip into beaten egg and then coat with the breadcrumbs mixed with the chopped almonds. Chill for at least 1 hour.

Heat the oil in a deep-fat fryer to 190 C/375 F or until a stale bread cube turns golden in 40-50 seconds. Lower a few of the croquettes carefully into the hot oil, then deep-fry for about 5 minutes until they are golden brown on all sides. Drain on kitchen paper and keep hot while frying the remainder. Serve immediately, garnished with parsley.

114 LEMON-GLAZED CARROTS

Preparation time:
5 minutes

Cooking time:
about 20 minutes

Serves 4

Calories:
101 per portion

**Suitable for vegans
using soya margarine**

YOU WILL NEED:

750 g/1 ½ lb new carrots, lightly
  scraped
juice of ½ lemon
½ teaspoon demerara sugar
25 g/1 oz butter or soya margarine
carrot tops or chopped parsley, to
  garnish

Put the carrots in a large saucepan and pour over the lemon juice and just enough boiling water to cover. Add the sugar and half of the butter, cover tightly and simmer for 15 minutes until the carrots are nearly tender.

Remove the lid and allow the liquid to evaporate completely. Turn into a warmed serving dish, top with remaining butter and garnish with carrot tops or parsley.

■ COOK'S TIP

*Add a sprinkling of nutmeg
to the croquettes for a spicy,
nutty flavour. Keep whole
nutmegs in an airtight jar
and grate them as required
on a miniature, fine grater.*

■ COOK'S TIP

*Choose bright orange carrots
without splits. Best eaten raw
for nutrition but if cooked
whole and scrubbed, not
peeled, they will still contain
plenty of Vitamin A.*

115 ITALIAN TOMATOES

Preparation time:
15 minutes

Cooking time:
15 minutes

Oven temperature:
200 C/400 F/gas 6

Serves 4

Calories:
153 per portion

YOU WILL NEED:
4 large tomatoes, halved
2 tablespoons oil
1 medium onion, finely chopped
2 garlic cloves, crushed
3-4 tablespoons fresh white
  breadcrumbs
1-2 tablespoons chopped fresh basil or
  parsley
salt and pepper
50 g/2 oz Gruyère cheese, grated
chopped parsley, to garnish

Scoop a little flesh from the centre of each tomato half.

Heat the oil in a medium pan, add the onion and garlic and cook until soft. Add the breadcrumbs, basil or parsley and salt and pepper to taste. Pile on top of each tomato half and cover with grated cheese. Place in an ovenproof dish.

Bake in a preheated oven for 10-15 minutes until the tomatoes are just cooked and the cheese brown. Garnish with chopped parsley.

116 BEAN AND BEANSPROUT STIR-FRY

Preparation time:
5 minutes

Cooking time:
about 10 minutes

Serves 4

Calories:
91 per portion

Suitable for vegans

YOU WILL NEED:
15 g/½ oz butter or soya margarine
  (see recipe 110)
1 tablespoon olive oil
275 g/10 oz French beans, or frozen
  whole green beans
275 g/10 oz beansprouts
salt and pepper
2 teaspoons paprika

Heat the butter or soya margarine and oil in a wok or large frying pan until foamy, then add the beans and stir-fry gently for about 4 minutes.

Push them to the sides of the wok, turn the heat up a little and add the beansprouts. Stir-fry for about 2 minutes.

Now mix the beans and beansprouts together adding a little salt, plenty of black pepper and the paprika. Stir-fry for 1 minute more, then turn into a warm serving dish and serve. Alternatively, serve straight from the wok.

■ COOK'S TIP

Choose any variety of cheese instead of Gruyère – Mozzarella has a particular affinity with tomatoes and basil. Vegetarian Cheddar or Red Leicester are good, too.

■ COOK'S TIP

Stir-frying is an excellent method of cooking vegetables. Quickly cooked in their own juices, the vegetables keep most of their nutritional content. If fresh *beans are used, blanch them in boiling water for 1 minute then drain before stir-frying.*

SALADS

Fresh, raw crunchy vegetables such as celery, carrots and peppers mingle well with soft and juicy varieties including tomatoes, avocado and beetroot. Sharp, tangy fruit such as apples, grapefruit and orange add the perfect contrast. Add cubes of cheese, chopped nuts or yogurt dressing for a filling meal. In this chapter is an array of higher and low-fat salad dressings to make nutritious and unusual creative dishes.

117 CHICORY, ORANGE AND WATERCRESS SALAD

Preparation time:	YOU WILL NEED:
15 minutes	2 heads of chicory, washed
	½ bunch watercress
Serves 4	2 small oranges, peeled and cut into
	slices
Calories:	FOR THE DRESSING
83 per portion	50 g/2 oz vegetarian Danish blue or
	Roquefort cheese, crumbled
	4 tablespoons soured cream

Arrange the chicory leaves and sprigs of watercress alternately in a circle with the leaf tips pointing outwards, like the spokes of a wheel, on a large serving dish or two individual plates. Put the orange slices in the centre, also in a circular pattern.

Make the dressing by mixing together the cheese and soured cream. Pour the dressing into the centre of the salad over the orange slices.

118 OKRA SALAD WITH VINAIGRETTE DRESSING

Preparation time:	YOU WILL NEED:
20 minutes	350-400 g/12-14 oz okra, trimmed
	juice of ½ lemon
Cooking time:	salt
15 minutes	FOR THE DRESSING
Serves 4	2 tablespoons olive oil
	1 garlic clove, crushed
Calories:	1 onion, finely chopped
101 per portion	2 teaspoons lemon juice
Suitable for vegans	6 tablespoons dry white wine
	freshly ground black pepper
	½ teaspoon French mustard

Bring 300 ml/½ pint water to the boil in a pan. Add the okra, lemon juice and salt, then bring back to the boil, lower the heat and cook for about 10 minutes. Drain and leave to cool.

To make the dressing, beat the oil with the garlic, onion, lemon juice, white wine, salt and pepper to taste and the mustard.

Cut each okra in half and place in a salad bowl. Pour over the vinaigrette dressing and toss well to mix. Cover and chill in the refrigerator for about 5-10 minutes, to allow the flavours to develop. Toss again before serving.

■ COOK'S TIP

If soured cream isn't available, use ordinary double or whipping cream instead and add ½ teaspoon lemon juice to the dressing.

■ COOK'S TIP

Always use fresh lemon juice, which has a high vitamin C content. If lemon juice is allowed to get stale, most of its nutritional properties are lost.

119 COUNTRY-STYLE TOMATO PLATTER

Preparation time:
20 minutes

Serves 4-6

Calories:
179-119 per portion

YOU WILL NEED:
750 g/1 ½ lb beef tomatoes, cut into thick slices
salt and pepper
1 onion, chopped
300 ml/ ½ pint soured cream
1 basil sprig, chopped
basil leaves, to garnish

Arrange the tomato slices on a flat serving dish and season with salt and pepper to taste. Scatter the onion evenly over the tomatoes. Mix the soured cream with the basil, blending well. Using a teaspoon, place a dot of cream on each tomato slice. Garnish with basil leaves before serving.

120 CELERY SALAD FLAVIA

Preparation time:
20 minutes, plus chilling

Serves 4

Calories:
117 per portion

Suitable for vegans

YOU WILL NEED:
1 garlic clove, halved
1 head celery, cut into small strips
1 × 200 g/7 oz can artichoke hearts in brine, drained and halved
1 tablespoon black olives, stoned
1 tablespoon chopped parsley
FOR THE DRESSING
3 tablespoons olive oil
1 tablespoon lemon juice
dash of Tabasco sauce
½ teaspoon made mustard
pinch of dried oregano
salt
few celery leaves, to garnish

Using the cut side of the garlic, vigorously rub the inside of a salad bowl, then discard. Add the celery, artichoke hearts, olives and parsley to the bowl.

To make the dressing, beat the olive oil with the lemon juice, Tabasco sauce, mustard, oregano and salt to taste.

Pour the dressing over the salad and toss well. Cover and chill for 30 minutes to allow the flavours to develop.

Toss the salad again before serving and garnish with a few celery leaves.

■ COOK'S TIP

The Italian olive bread called ciabatta makes an ideal accompaniment for this salad. Buy the ready-to-bake version and serve fresh from the oven.

■ COOK'S TIP

For special occasions, this salad can be garnished with a ring of hard-boiled egg slices and tomato wedges. Note, though, that egg is not suitable for vegans.

121 PALM HEART SALAD WITH DILL MAYONNAISE

Preparation time:
20 minutes, plus
standing

Serves 4

Calories:
127 per portion

YOU WILL NEED:
1 × 425 g/15 oz can palm hearts,
*   drained*
2 hard-boiled eggs, shelled and finely
*   chopped*
FOR THE DRESSING
1 tablespoon mayonnaise
4-5 tablespoons soured cream
pinch of cayenne pepper
1-2 teaspoons chopped dill

Cut the palm hearts into 2.5 cm/1 inch lengths. Spread the chopped eggs over the palm hearts and place in a serving dish.

To make the dressing, beat the mayonnaise with the soured cream, cayenne pepper and dill. Pour the dressing over the palm hearts and toss well to mix. Leave to stand for about 10 minutes to allow the flavours to develop.

122 SPRING ONION AND MUSHROOM SALAD

Preparation time:
20 minutes, plus
standing

Serves 4

Calories:
95 per portion

YOU WILL NEED:
1 bunch spring onions
1 orange
1 red pepper, cored, seeded and cut
*   into strips*
100 g/4 oz button mushrooms, halved
FOR THE DRESSING
3 tablespoons dry white wine
1 tablespoon snipped chives
120 ml/4 fl oz soured cream
salt and pepper

Trim the roots from the spring onions and cut both the white and green stems into fine rings. Place the rings in a sieve, rinse and drain thoroughly.

Peel and segment the orange, removing all pith. Mix the spring onions with the orange segments, pepper strips and mushrooms in a serving bowl.

To make the dressing, beat the white wine with the chives, soured cream and salt and pepper to taste. Pour over the salad and toss well to mix.

Leave the salad to stand for about 30 minutes before serving to allow the flavours to develop.

■ COOK'S TIP

Palm heart salad makes an appetising hors d'oeuvre or vegetable dish. Canned palm hearts are now widely available from supermarkets. They are a luxury because *when these tender shoots are cut off the tree, it dies.*

■ COOK'S TIP

Serve in individual dishes with buttered toast as an unusual light starter or side salad. Use natural yogurt instead of soured cream for a lower fat version.

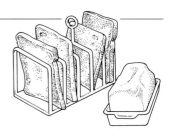

123 RADISH AND CUCUMBER SALAD

Preparation time:	YOU WILL NEED:
20 minutes	1 Daikon radish (see Cook's Tip)
	½ cucumber
Serves 4	salt
Calories:	FOR THE DRESSING
105 per portion	1 tablespoon white wine vinegar
	3 tablespoons sunflower oil
Suitable for vegans	1 sprig of dill, finely chopped

Peel and grate the radish. Peel and thinly slice the cucumber. Place in a bowl, sprinkle with a little salt, mix thoroughly and leave to stand for 10 minutes. Rinse and drain thoroughly. Place in a serving bowl.

To make the dressing, beat the wine vinegar with the oil and dill. Pour over the salad and toss well to mix. Serve as a side salad.

124 WATERCRESS AND EGG SALAD

Preparation time:	YOU WILL NEED:
30 minutes	2 bunches watercress
	FOR THE DRESSING
Serves 4	120 ml/4 fl oz soured cream
Calories:	1 garlic clove, crushed with salt
127 per portion	1 tablespoon chopped fresh parsley
	1 tomato, skinned and chopped
	2 hard-boiled eggs, shelled and chopped
	freshly ground black pepper
	FOR THE GARNISH
	1 tomato, cut in wedges
	1 hard-boiled egg, shelled and sliced

Trim the watercress stems, sort the leaves, place in a sieve, rinse and drain.

To make the dressing, mix the soured cream and garlic together. Fold in the parsley, tomato and chopped egg. Season with pepper to taste.

Arrange the watercress in a serving bowl and top with the egg and tomato dressing. Garnish with the tomato wedges and the sliced egg.

■ COOK'S TIP

The Daikon, or Japanese radish, is milder than the red radish, and delicious raw or cooked. Radishes are good sources of calcium, iron and vitamin C.

■ COOK'S TIP

For a special Easter variation, fill a bowl with watercress marinated in a vinaigrette dressing. Top with halved hard-boiled quail's eggs or hard-boiled *eggs in their shells, coloured by soaking in beetroot juice.*

125 CELERIAC AND FRUIT SALAD

Preparation time:
20 minutes

Serves 4

Calories:
106 per portion

YOU WILL NEED:
2-3 dessert apples
2 bananas
1 small celeriac, peeled and cut into
*   strips*
2 tablespoons chopped walnuts
FOR THE DRESSING
2 tablespoons lemon juice
pinch of salt
pinch of ground allspice
2 tablespoons double cream

Peel, core and slice the apples. Peel the bananas and cut into chunks. Mix the apple with the banana, celeriac and walnuts in a serving bowl.

For the dressing, mix the lemon juice with the salt and allspice and immediately stir into the salad. Add the cream and toss the ingredients well to mix. Serve immediately with buttered wholemeal bread.

126 RADICCHIO AND FRENCH BEAN SALAD

Preparation time:
15 minutes

Cooking time:
10 minutes

Serves 4-6

Calories:
175-116 per portion

Suitable for vegans

YOU WILL NEED:
350 g/12 oz French beans, trimmed
salt
1 head radicchio
1 onion, sliced into rings
FOR THE DRESSING
2 garlic cloves, crushed
4-5 tablespoons olive oil
2-3 slices white bread, crusts removed

Parboil the French beans in boiling, salted water for 2 minutes; rinse and drain. Cut into 5 cm/2 inch lengths.

Separate the radicchio, place the leaves in a sieve, rinse and drain thoroughly. Tear into large pieces and place in a salad bowl with the French beans and onion rings.

To make the dressing, beat the garlic with the olive oil and a pinch of salt. Pour two-thirds of the dressing over the salad and mix thoroughly.

Cut the bread into cubes. Heat the remaining dressing in a frying pan over a high heat, add the bread cubes and fry until golden brown. Drain on absorbent kitchen paper. Sprinkle the bread cubes over the salad and serve immediately as a snack or part of a buffet spread.

■ COOK'S TIP

The uneven surface of celeriac makes it difficult to peel. If the root is first cut into thick slices, it is easier to remove the peel, using a small vegetable knife.

■ COOK'S TIP

Raw garlic is used in many salad dressings. It is best known for its ability not only to cleanse the blood but to reduce cholesterol. It may also help prevent colds.

127 RADICCHIO ROSETTE

Preparation time:
15 minutes

Serves 4

Calories:
207 per portion

Suitable for vegans

YOU WILL NEED:
1 head radicchio
2-3 tablespoons Italian dressing (see Cook's Tip)
½ fennel bulb, cut into fine julienne strips
2 teaspoons lemon juice
6-8 black olives, stoned (optional)

Rinse and drain the radicchio without removing the thick stem. Carefully prise the leaves apart with your fingers to form a rosette, being careful not to break the leaves off the stem.

Holding the radicchio firmly by the stem, dip the leaves into the Italian dressing several times to coat. Carefully cut away the stem and place the radicchio rosette in a serving bowl.

Toss the fennel in the lemon juice to prevent discoloration. Fill the middle of the radicchio rosette with the fennel and olives, if using. Sprinkle the remaining fennel on top to serve.

128 ICEBERG LETTUCE WITH HAZELNUTS

Preparation time:
20 minutes, plus standing

Serves 4

Calories:
210 per portion

Suitable for vegans

YOU WILL NEED:
1 small iceberg lettuce
1 carrot, grated
2-3 tablespoons coarsely chopped hazelnuts (see Cook's Tip)
FOR THE DRESSING
3 tablespoons olive oil
2 tablespoons lemon juice
1 teaspoon made mustard
salt and pepper
few avocado slices (sprinkled with lemon juice) or cucumber slices, to garnish

Tear the lettuce into large pieces or strips, place in a sieve, rinse and drain thoroughly. Arrange in a serving bowl. Top with the grated carrot and hazelnuts.

To make the dressing, beat the oil with the lemon juice, mustard, and salt and pepper to taste, until smooth. Pour the dressing evenly over the salad. Cover and leave to stand in the refrigerator for a few minutes before serving, to allow the flavours to develop.

Garnish with avocado or cucumber slices before serving.

■ COOK'S TIP

For the Italian dressing, combine 1 tablespoon lemon juice, 1 tablespoon white wine vinegar, 6 tablespoons olive oil, 1 crushed garlic clove, 1 tablespoon chopped fresh basil or oregano, seasoning and a pinch of sugar. Stir well.

■ COOK'S TIP

To bring out the nutty flavour of the hazelnuts, toast in a moderate oven for about 10 minutes until golden brown. Cool slightly before chopping.

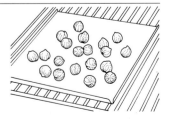

129 CALIFORNIAN SALAD

Preparation time:
15 minutes

Serves 4 as a main course

Calories:
394 per portion

YOU WILL NEED:
1 kg/2 lb assorted fruit (choose from
    apricots, fresh cherries, grapefruit,
    kiwi fruit, melon, nectarines, peaches,
    raspberries and strawberries)
50 g/2 oz chopped nuts
2 bananas
1 tablespoon lemon juice
450 g/1 lb vegetarian cottage cheese

Prepare all the fruit (except the bananas), peeling, slicing, stoning and hulling as necessary. Combine all the prepared fruit in a large bowl.

Toast the nuts under a preheated medium grill for 2 minutes until lightly browned.

Peel the bananas, cut into long diagonal slices and immediately toss in the lemon juice to prevent discoloration. Add the banana slices to the other fruit.

Spoon the cottage cheese into the centre of the fruit in the bowl and sprinkle the chopped nuts over it. Serve immediately.

130 GREEN AND WHITE SALAD

Preparation time:
8 minutes

Serves 4

Calories:
about 40 per portion

YOU WILL NEED:
400 g/14 oz young turnips, no more
    than 5 cm/2 inches across, peeled
50 g/2 oz roughly chopped fresh parsley
4 tablespoons cultured buttermilk or
    natural yogurt
1 tablespoon lemon juice
1 tablespoon chopped fresh chives
pinch of salt (optional)
freshly ground black pepper
paprika, for dusting (optional)

Cut the peeled turnips into paper-thin slices directly into a serving bowl.

Stir in all the remaining ingredients except the paprika.

Dust lightly with paprika if liked, just before serving.

■ COOK'S TIP

This healthy and hearty salad is packed with protein, calcium and vitamins, especially vitamin C. It's also low in fat and an excellent source of fibre.

■ COOK'S TIP

Small, young turnips are tender and deliciously sweet. They will keep in a cool, dry place for quite some time. Try grating them for a different texture.

131 APRICOT AND APPLE SALAD

Preparation time:
15 minutes, plus
soaking

Serves 4

Calories:
330 per portion

YOU WILL NEED:
175 g/6 oz dried apricots
200 ml/7 fl oz cloudy apple juice
3 dessert apples, cored and thinly sliced
3 tender celery sticks, thinly sliced
3 tablespoons walnut halves
celery leaves, to garnish
FOR THE DRESSING
3 tablespoons olive oil
3 tablespoons cloudy apple juice
2 tablespoons pumpkin seeds
salt and pepper

Soak the dried apricots in the apple juice for about 2 hours. Stir in the sliced apples, celery and walnuts.

Mix together the dressing ingredients. Pour the dressing over the fruit mixture and toss well.

Spoon the salad on to a serving dish and garnish it with the celery leaves.

132 LETTUCE AND FRESH HERB SALAD

Preparation time:
15 minutes

Serves 4

Calories:
110 per portion

Suitable for vegans

YOU WILL NEED:
1 tablespoon Dijon mustard
½ teaspoon sugar
1 tablespoon red wine vinegar
3 tablespoons olive oil
salt and pepper
½ small cucumber, peeled and thinly sliced
1 small hearty lettuce, shredded
2 tablespoons chopped mixed herbs (see Cook's Tip)

Mix together the mustard, sugar, red wine vinegar and oil. Season with salt and pepper and add the cucumber, lettuce and herbs just before serving.

■ COOK'S TIP

Dried apricots are not only a good source of fibre, they have a high iron content. Soaking them before use makes them much easier to digest.

■ COOK'S TIP

Use any combination of chopped mixed herbs such as parsley, basil, dill, chervil, oregano, coriander or marjoram.

133 SHREDDED SPINACH WITH MUSHROOMS

Preparation time:
15 minutes

Serves 4

Calories:
124 per portion

Suitable for vegans

YOU WILL NEED:
1 tablespoon Dijon mustard
1 tablespoon white wine vinegar
1 garlic clove, crushed
½ teaspoon salt
3 tablespoons olive oil
450 g/1 lb tender spinach leaves,
    washed and finely shredded
100 g/4 oz button mushrooms, sliced
    (see Cook's Tip)

Put the mustard, vinegar, garlic and salt into a bowl. Gradually stir in the oil to make a thick dressing, then add the spinach and mushrooms and stir gently, until all the ingredients are well coated.

134 CRISP WINTER SALAD

Preparation time:
8 minutes

Serves 4

Calories:
71 per portion

YOU WILL NEED:
40 g/1 ½ oz flaked almonds
225 g/8 oz celery, thinly sliced
1 large orange, peeled, segmented and
    roughly chopped
150 ml/¼ pint natural yogurt
1 teaspoon ground coriander (optional)
½ teaspoon ground cumin or fennel
    seed
pinch of salt (optional)

Place the almonds in an ungreased heavy-based frying pan over a low heat for 2-3 minutes, stirring until slightly browned.

Put half the almonds with the prepared celery and orange in a serving bowl and toss lightly.

Mix together the yogurt, coriander (if using) and cumin or fennel seed. Pour this dressing over the salad. Taste and add a little salt if necessary.

Sprinkle the remaining almonds over the salad and serve.

▨ COOK'S TIP

It is not necessary to peel mushrooms unless the skin is blemished. Just place in a sieve and rinse under a trickling tap or wipe with a damp cloth.

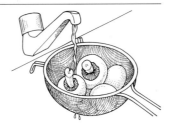

▨ COOK'S TIP

A crunchy combination of textures, sweetened with orange and spices, makes this salad a contrast to the rather stodgy or heavy nature of much winter food.

135 WALDORF SALAD

Preparation time:
10 minutes

Serves 6-8

Calories:
285-214 per portion

YOU WILL NEED:
150 ml/ ¼ pint mayonnaise (see Cook's Tip)
2 tablespoons natural yogurt
3 dessert apples, cored and chopped
4 sticks celery, chopped
25 g/1 oz walnut pieces
chopped fresh parsley, to garnish

Mix the mayonnaise and yogurt together in a bowl. Add the apples, celery and walnuts and toss well to coat with mayonnaise.

Pile the salad on to a shallow serving dish and sprinkle with the parsley.

136 MOROCCAN SALAD

Preparation time:
10 minutes

Serves 4

Calories:
120 per portion

YOU WILL NEED:
25 g/1 oz blanched split almonds (see recipe 32)
1 bunch watercress, coarse stems removed, washed and roughly chopped
2 large oranges, about 275 g/10 oz flesh, peeled and thinly sliced
100 g/4 oz vegetarian cottage cheese
50 g/2 oz fresh or dried dates, roughly chopped
1 teaspoon ground coriander (optional)

Grill the blanched split almonds on an ungreased baking sheet for 2-3 minutes, shaking to turn them so that they brown evenly on all sides.

Arrange the prepared watercress and orange slices around the inside edge of a serving dish.

Either stir in the cottage cheese, or place it in a neat mound in the dish. Arrange the dates and toasted almonds on top.

Sprinkle the salad with the coriander (if using) and serve.

COOK'S TIP

To make your own mayonnaise, beat together 1 egg yolk with ¼ teaspoon each salt, pepper and dry mustard. Add 150 ml/ ¼ pint olive oil drop by drop, beating constantly. As it thickens, add the oil in a steady stream. Add 1 tablespoon white wine vinegar and mix thoroughly.

COOK'S TIP

Watercress, available all year round, has a spicy rather bitter taste and works well in salads. It has a reasonable iron content as well as vitamins A and C.

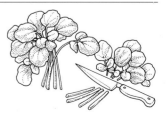

137 CALIFORNIAN ICEBERG LETTUCE SALAD

Preparation time:
15 minutes

Serves 4

Calories:
170 per portion

YOU WILL NEED:
½ iceberg lettuce
2 hard-boiled eggs, shelled and quartered
2 tablespoons salad cress
2 tablespoons mayonnaise (see recipe 135)
120 ml/4 fl oz soured cream
few stuffed olives, sliced
1 tablespoon chopped onion
1 teaspoon chilli sauce
salt
tomato wedges, to garnish

Cut the lettuce into wedges or tear the leaves into large strips. Place in a sieve, rinse and drain thoroughly. Arrange in a salad bowl. Mix in the eggs and cress.

To make the dressing, mix the mayonnaise with the soured cream, olives, onion, chilli sauce, and salt to taste. Pour the dressing over the salad and serve immediately, garnished with tomato wedges.

138 COTTAGE COLESLAW

Preparation time:
15 minutes

Serves 4 as a main course

Calories:
260 per portion

YOU WILL NEED:
225 g/8 oz white cabbage, finely shredded
225 g/8 oz carrots, coarsely shredded
3 sticks celery, finely sliced
1 bunch watercress, base of stems removed, chopped
100 g/4 oz green-skinned apple, diced
2 teaspoons lemon or orange juice
50 g/2 oz sultanas
50 g/2 oz hazelnuts, toasted and chopped (see recipe 128)
150 ml/¼ pint natural yogurt
1 teaspoon white wine vinegar
½ teaspoon dried tarragon or crushed caraway seeds
salt and pepper
450 g/1 lb vegetarian cottage cheese

Mix all the ingredients except the cottage cheese in a large bowl, making sure the apple is quickly coated in the lemon or orange juice.

Spoon the cottage cheese on to the other ingredients in the bowl and mix well. Serve immediately.

■ COOK'S TIP

Instead of iceberg lettuce, try using cos, or romaine, lettuce. It has a delicious taste and crunchy texture. Try topping the salad with croûtons if liked.

■ COOK'S TIP

This dish is low in calories and fat. Add some mayonnaise instead of yogurt if you feel like an indulgence!

139 TRICOLOUR SALAD

Preparation time:
10 minutes

Serves 4

Calories:
about 55 per portion

YOU WILL NEED:
100 g/4 oz leeks, trimmed and sliced
  into rings
100 g/4 oz red pepper, cored, seeded
  and sliced
2 medium oranges, about 225 g/8 oz
  flesh, peeled and cut into quartered
  slices
FOR THE DRESSING
1 tablespoon chopped fresh dill
1 tablespoon chopped fresh parsley
150 ml/¼ pint natural yogurt
1 teaspoon clear honey
freshly ground black pepper

Combine the prepared leeks, red pepper and oranges in a serving dish or salad bowl.

Blend together the dill, parsley, yogurt, honey and pepper and pour over the salad.

140 GRAPEFRUIT AND AVOCADO WITH MINTY DRESSING

Preparation time:
25 minutes

Serves 4

Calories:
353 per portion

Suitable for vegans

YOU WILL NEED:
2 avocados, halved, peeled and stones
  removed
2 grapefruits
2 oranges
6-10 lettuce leaves, washed and torn
  into bite-sized pieces, or 2 heads of
  chicory, washed and leaves separated
dressing (see Cook's Tip)

Cut the avocados into thin slices. Spread the slices out on a plate. Holding a grapefruit over the plate (so that the juice will go over the avocado slices), peel it with a sharp knife. Do this with a sawing action, cutting round the fruit down to the flesh and removing all the white pith. Then cut each segment of fruit away from the inner white skin. When all the segments have been removed from the grapefruit, squeeze the remaining juice from the skin over the avocados. Repeat this with the other grapefruit and the oranges, putting the segments on a separate plate. Turn the avocado slices in the juice, then drain off any excess juice into a small bowl for the dressing.

To assemble the dish, cover six plates with lettuce or chicory leaves, then arrange segments of grapefruit, orange and avocado on top, dividing them between the plates. Make the dressing (see Cook's Tip), give it a quick stir then spoon a little over each salad.

■ COOK'S TIP

Bright colours and contrasting textures make this salad a refreshing antidote to the end of winter. For the best flavour, serve at room temperature.

■ COOK'S TIP

For the dressing, to the excess juice add ½ teaspoon sugar, 2 tablespoons olive oil, 1 tablespoon chopped mint and seasoning. Stir well before serving.

141 CELERIAC WITH LEMON-MUSTARD DRESSING

Preparation time:
10 minutes

Serves 4

Calories:
58 per portion

YOU WILL NEED:
½ teaspoon mustard powder
3 tablespoons lemon juice
½ teaspoon clear honey
¼ teaspoon freshly ground black
   pepper
150 ml/¼ pint natural yogurt
pinch of salt
450 g/1 lb peeled celeriac (see recipe
   125)
1 carrot, coarsely shredded
¼ teaspoon paprika

Blend together the mustard, lemon juice, honey, pepper, yogurt and salt and pour into a shallow serving dish.

Shred the celeriac very coarsely directly into the mixture to prevent discoloration. Stir in the carrot.

Sprinkle with the paprika and serve.

142 JACKET POTATO SALAD

Preparation time:
5 minutes

Cooking time:
30-45 minutes

Oven temperature:
200 C/400 F/gas 6

Serves 4

Calories:
111 per portion

YOU WILL NEED:
350 g/12 oz small potatoes, scrubbed
2-3 spring onions, trimmed and finely
   chopped
150 ml/¼ pint natural yogurt
2 tablespoons lemon juice
1 teaspoon English mustard
salt and pepper
175 g/6 oz red peppers, cored, seeded
   and roughly sliced

Thread the potatoes on to metal kebab skewers. Bake in a preheated oven for about 30 minutes or until tender.

Stir all the remaining ingredients, except the peppers, together in a serving dish.

Allow the potatoes to cool slightly, then cut into rough quarters or cubes and add to the dish with the peppers. Toss well and serve.

■ COOK'S TIP

The unattractive knobbly exterior of celeriac hides a distinctive and delicious celery-like flavour, which blends perfectly with lemon and mustard.

■ COOK'S TIP

A home-made English mustard adds a sharp flavour to this salad. As an alternative, use Dijon mustard which will give a milder, sweeter flavour.

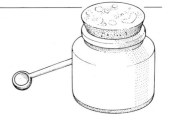

143 CARROT, TURNIP AND SESAME SEED SALAD

Preparation time:
20 minutes

Serves 4-6

Calories:
408–272 per portion

YOU WILL NEED:
350 g/12 oz carrots
175 g/6 oz turnip
50 g/2 oz seedless raisins
2 tablespoons sesame seeds, toasted (see Cook's Tip)
2 tablespoons snipped chives
FOR THE DRESSING
150 ml/¼ pint olive oil
1 tablespoon white wine vinegar
2 tablespoons lemon juice
grated zest of 1 lemon
1 teaspoon French mustard
1 teaspoon honey
salt and pepper

Grate the carrot and turnip finely and place in a salad bowl. Add the raisins, sesame seeds and chives. Toss well. Mix together all the dressing ingredients and pour 4 tablespoons over the salad.

144 BEETROOT AND ORANGE SALAD

Preparation time:
20 minutes

Serves 4

Calories:
136 per portion

YOU WILL NEED:
450 g/1 lb cooked beetroot, skinned
150 ml/¼ pint soured cream
1 medium orange
2 tablespoons chopped fresh chives
salt and pepper
chopped fresh chives, to garnish

Cut the beetroot into dice about 1 cm/½ inch square and arrange in a shallow serving dish.

Put the soured cream into a mixing bowl. Add the grated zest and juice from half the orange. Cut the peel and pith away from the remaining orange half and cut the flesh into segments. Scatter the orange segments over the beetroot.

Mix the chives and salt and pepper to taste with the soured cream. Pour this dressing over the beetroot and orange, but do not stir. Sprinkle with more chives and serve at once.

■ COOK'S TIP

To toast the sesame seeds, shake them in a heavy-based pan over a moderate heat for a minute or two. They could also be put in a frying pan under a moderate grill, shaking to turn them, until golden brown.

■ COOK'S TIP

Remember always to use a glass or china bowl for salads using beetroot. The juice will stain a wooden bowl. Also, do not use wooden salad servers.

145 HELIOS SALAD

Preparation time:
10 minutes

Serves 4

Calories:
96 per portion

YOU WILL NEED:
450 g/1 lb carrots, coarsely shredded
25 g/1 oz walnut pieces
120 ml/4 fl oz unsweetened apple juice
120 ml/4 fl oz natural yogurt
½ teaspoon mixed spice
1 peach, stoned and roughly chopped

Place the shredded carrots in a serving dish.

Blend the walnuts with half the apple juice in a liquidizer, leaving some walnut pieces intact to give a nutty texture. Transfer to a small bowl.

By hand, stir in the remaining apple juice, yogurt and mixed spice. Stir the mixture and the chopped peach into the carrots and serve.

146 CREAMY COLESLAW

Preparation time:
20 minutes

Serves 6

Calories:
140 per portion

YOU WILL NEED:
450 g/1 lb white cabbage, finely
   shredded
225 g/8 oz carrots, coarsely grated
2 onions, finely chopped
100 g/4 oz raisins
FOR THE DRESSING
1 teaspoon dry mustard
150 ml/¼ pint soured cream
salt and pepper

Put the cabbage, carrots, onions and raisins into a large bowl. In a small bowl, blend the mustard with the soured cream, and season to taste with salt and pepper. Add the dressing to the salad, mixing them well together. Check the seasoning before serving the coleslaw.

■ COOK'S TIP

Walnuts tend to turn rancid quickly. Buy in small quantities and store in an airtight container in a cool, dry, dark cupboard or the refrigerator.

■ COOK'S TIP

Try a spicy yogurt dressing. Beat together 150 ml/¼ pint thick Greek yogurt, 1 teaspoon ground turmeric and 1 crushed garlic clove.

147 RED SALAD

Preparation time:
15 minutes

Serves 4

Calories:
121 per portion

YOU WILL NEED:
FOR THE DRESSING
½ teaspoon mustard powder
2 teaspoons honey
1 tablespoon red wine vinegar
3 tablespoons olive oil
salt and pepper
FOR THE SALAD
bunch of radishes, trimmed and sliced
1 radicchio (175-225 g/6-8 oz), washed,
  leaves separated
100-175 g/4-6 oz red cabbage, shredded
1 sweet red pepper, seeded and diced

For the dressing, put the mustard powder, honey, red wine vinegar, oil and a little salt and pepper into a salad bowl and mix well. Add the salad ingredients, and toss to coat the vegetables with the dressing. Serve at once.

148 CHRISTMAS COLESLAW

Preparation time:
30 minutes

Serves 4

Calories:
432 per portion

YOU WILL NEED:
100 g/4 oz red cabbage, finely shredded
100 g/4 oz white cabbage, finely
  shredded
2 dessert apples, preferably red-skinned,
  cored and thinly sliced
50 g/2 oz shelled nuts, chopped, e.g.
  walnuts, almonds or hazelnuts
150 ml/¼ pint mayonnaise
2 tablespoons French dressing (see
  Cook's Tip)
fresh parsley leaves, to garnish

Mix together the prepared cabbages, apples and chopped nuts in a large bowl.

Mix the mayonnaise with the French dressing. Pour over the cabbage salad and toss until everything is thoroughly coated. Transfer to a serving dish and garnish with the fresh parsley.

■ COOK'S TIP

To garnish this dish, scatter over some thinly sliced red onion rings. They have a sweeter, milder flavour than ordinary onions and an attractive colour.

■ COOK'S TIP

For the French dressing place in a screw-topped jar 5 tablespoons olive oil, 2 tablespoons white wine vinegar, 1 teaspoon Dijon mustard, 1 crushed clove *garlic, ½ teaspoon honey and salt and pepper to taste. Shake well before serving.*

149 MUSHROOM AND GRUYERE SALAD

Preparation time:
30 minutes, plus marinating

Serves 4

Calories:
438 per portion

YOU WILL NEED:
225 g/8 oz Gruyère cheese, cut into small cubes
100 g/4 oz button mushrooms, quartered
4 large lettuce leaves
1 tablespoon finely chopped fresh parsley
FOR THE DRESSING
6 tablespoons olive oil
2 tablespoons red wine vinegar
1 garlic clove, crushed
½ teaspoon salt
large pinch of freshly ground black pepper

Put all the dressing ingredients in a screw-topped jar and shake until well mixed.

Place the cheese and mushrooms in a mixing bowl and pour over the dressing. Toss to coat and leave for 20 minutes.

Line a shallow salad bowl with the lettuce leaves. Spoon the cheese mixture on top of the lettuce and sprinkle with the chopped parsley. Serve at once.

150 CARROT AND APPLE SALAD

Preparation time:
20 minutes

Serves 4

Calories:
351 per portion

Suitable for vegans

YOU WILL NEED:
350 g/12 oz carrots, scraped and coarsely grated
3 Cox's Orange Pippin apples, cored and sliced
1 tablespoon lemon juice
1 tablespoon sunflower seeds
3 tablespoons raisins
2 teaspoons vegetable oil
2 tablespoons cashew nuts
FOR THE FRENCH DRESSING
4 tablespoons vegetable oil
2 ½ tablespoons cider vinegar or lemon juice
pinch of caster sugar
salt and pepper

Put the grated carrot into a large bowl. Sprinkle the apple slices with lemon juice to prevent them discolouring, then add to the bowl with the sunflower seeds and raisins.

Heat the oil in a small pan and lightly brown the cashew nuts. Lift out and drain on absorbent kitchen paper, then add to the bowl.

Put all the dressing ingredients in a screw-topped jar and shake well to mix. Spoon over the salad and toss lightly.

■ COOK'S TIP

If you find wine vinegar rather too sharp for your taste, try balsamic vinegar instead. It has a rich, sweet flavour. Raspberry vinegar is another alternative.

■ COOK'S TIP

This salad is also delicious served with Greek or natural yogurt instead of the dressing. Add other nuts for variety. Sprinkle with toasted sesame seeds, if liked.

151 PIQUANT POTATO SALAD

Preparation time:
5 minutes, plus cooling

Cooking time:
15-20 minutes

Serves 4

Calories:
206 per portion

Suitable for vegans

YOU WILL NEED:
750 g/1 ½ lb tiny new potatoes
salt
FOR THE DRESSING
3 tablespoons olive oil
1 tablespoon white wine vinegar
freshly ground black pepper
½ teaspoon made English mustard
2 teaspoons capers, finely chopped
1 pickled gherkin, finely chopped
1 tablespoon chopped fresh parsley

Wash the potatoes and place in a pan of boiling, salted water. Cook for 15-20 minutes until just tender.

While the potatoes are cooking prepare the dressing. Put the oil and vinegar into a small bowl and stir in the salt, pepper, mustard, capers and gherkin. Add the chopped parsley.

Drain the potatoes well and tip them into a bowl. Pour the dressing over the hot potatoes and stir gently to coat them all thoroughly. Leave to cool, but do not chill. Serve in a shallow dish at room temperature.

152 WINTER VEGETABLE SALAD

Preparation time:
1 hour

Serves 6

Calories:
221 per portion

Suitable for vegans

YOU WILL NEED:
4 medium waxy potatoes, peeled,
  cooked and diced
1 large celery stick, finely chopped
2 carrots, scraped and grated
1 small onion, finely chopped
½ small white cabbage, cored and
  shredded
2 tablespoons chopped pickled gherkins
8 black olives, stoned and chopped
FOR THE DRESSING
5 tablespoons olive or other salad oil
3-4 tablespoons lemon juice
1 teaspoon Dijon mustard
salt and pepper

Put the potatoes, celery, carrots, onion, cabbage, gherkins and olives in a salad bowl.

Put all the dressing ingredients in a screw-topped jar and shake well. Adjust the seasoning, pour the dressing over the vegetables and toss well.

■ COOK'S TIP

This salad could also be served warm. Stir in a chopped hard-boiled egg or some walnuts for extra protein (though eggs are not suitable for vegans).

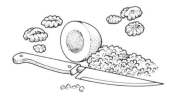

■ COOK'S TIP

Fennel with its aniseed flavour may be finely chopped and substituted for the celery in this dish. Peeled and grated celeriac also tastes good.

RICE & PASTA

Rice and pasta are both excellent protein and fibre sources. They can be served with an infinite variety of sauces, vegetables, fruits and nuts. Although the pasta recipes here are based mostly on dried varieties, experiment with fresh types, such as tagliatelle or spaghetti, for a quicker-cooking dish.

153 RICE-STUFFED PEPPERS

Preparation time:
25 minutes

Cooking time:
1 hour 25 minutes

Oven temperature:
190 C/375 F/gas 5

Serves 4

Calories:
260 per portion

YOU WILL NEED:
2 tablespoons olive oil
225 g/8 oz long-grain rice
8 tablespoons vegetable stock (recipe 3)
275 g/10 oz fresh spinach, trimmed
175 g/6 oz Feta cheese, crumbled
25 g/1 oz basil or mint, chopped
2 teaspoons dried dill
1 egg, beaten
freshly ground black pepper
8 red, green or yellow peppers
2 tablespoons lemon juice

Heat 1 tablespoon of the oil over a gentle heat, add the rice and toss until thoroughly coated. Add the vegetable stock. Simmer uncovered until all the liquid has been absorbed. The rice will now only be partially cooked.

Finely chop the spinach and mix it with the crumbled Feta cheese, basil, dill and beaten egg. Add pepper to taste, and combine with the cooled rice.

Wipe the peppers and cut off the tops to make lids. Use scissors to snip down and inside to loosen all the seeds, but take care not to pierce the sides. Remove the seeds.

Fill each pepper with the rice mixture, replace the lids and stand them, tightly packed together, in a casserole with a lid. Trickle over the remaining tablespoon of oil and the lemon juice and add enough water to come two-thirds of the way up the sides of the casserole. Cover and bake in a preheated oven for about 1¼ hours. Serve warm or cold.

154 FRUIT AND NUT PILAFF

Preparation time:
20 minutes, plus soaking

Cooking time:
40 minutes

Oven temperature:
190 C/375 F/gas 5

Serves 6

Calories:
366 per portion

YOU WILL NEED:
75 g/3 oz sultanas
175 g/6 oz dried fruit (apricots, apples, pears, etc.)
1 tablespoon sweet sherry
75 g/3 oz butter
1 onion, finely chopped
225 g/8 oz brown rice, cooked (see recipe 155)
½ teaspoon ground allspice
salt and pepper
50 g/2 oz flaked almonds

Put the sultanas and dried fruit in a bowl, sprinkle with the sherry and cover with water. Leave to soak for 4 hours. Drain and chop the apricots, apples or pears.

Melt the butter in a frying pan, add the onion and fry until softened. Stir in the rice and allspice, then add salt and pepper to taste and mix well.

Fold in the fruit and almonds, then turn the mixture into a greased casserole. Bake in a preheated moderately hot oven for 30 minutes.

■ COOK'S TIP

As a variation, use Mozzarella or vegetarian Gruyère cheese instead of the Feta. This filling is also a good one for using to stuff vine leaves.

■ COOK'S TIP

This sweet, spicy dish is packed with protein, vitamins and minerals. It is also high in fibre. Serve with a crisp salad for a nutritious lunch.

155 SPICED VEGETABLES AND RICE

Preparation time:
20 minutes

Cooking time:
50 minutes

Serves 2

Calories:
312 per portion

Suitable for vegans

YOU WILL NEED:
1 tablespoon oil
1 leek, sliced
1 carrot, thinly sliced
1 onion, sliced
½ dessert apple, cored and chopped
½ teaspoon cumin seeds
½ teaspoon ground coriander
pinch of cayenne pepper
salt and pepper
4-5 tablespoons vegetable stock (see recipe 3)
100 g/4 oz brown rice
chopped parsley, to garnish

Heat the oil in a saucepan, add the leek, carrot, onion and apple and cook gently, stirring, for 3 minutes. Add the cumin, coriander, cayenne and salt and pepper to taste. Continue to cook for 3 minutes, then stir in the stock. Cover and simmer for 10-15 minutes until the vegetables are tender but not soft.

Cook the rice in plenty of boiling, salted water for 25–30 minutes or until tender. Drain and rinse with boiling water.

Stir the rice into the vegetables and heat gently for 5 minutes. Transfer to a warmed serving dish and garnish with parsley. Serve hot.

156 TAGLIATELLE VERDE WITH MUSHROOMS

Preparation time:
20 minutes

Cooking time:
30 minutes

Serves 4

Calories:
484 per portion

YOU WILL NEED:
225-350 g/8-12 oz tagliatelle verde
FOR THE SAUCE
1 onion, chopped
40 g/1 ½ oz butter or margarine
1 garlic clove, crushed
350 g/12 oz button mushrooms, wiped and sliced
300 ml/ ½ pint soured cream
salt and pepper
freshly grated nutmeg
flat-leafed parsley or watercress sprigs, to garnish

First make the sauce: fry the onion gently in 25 g/1 oz butter or margarine for about 10 minutes until softened. Then add the garlic and mushrooms and cook quickly for 2-3 minutes. Add the soured cream, season with salt, pepper and nutmeg, then remove from the heat. Half-fill a large saucepan with water and bring to the boil, then add the tagliatelle. Stir once, then leave the tagliatelle to cook, uncovered, for 10-15 minutes, until a piece feels tender but not soggy when you bite it. Drain immediately into a colander, then tip back into the still hot saucepan, add the rest of the butter or margarine and some salt and pepper. Stir for 1 minute until the fat has melted. Quickly re-heat the sauce, then tip the tagliatelle into a hot serving dish. Pour the sauce over the top and serve at once garnished with flat-leafed parsley or watercress sprigs.

■ COOK'S TIP

Cumin is best bought in seed form and ground as needed. If bought ready-ground, get only a small quantity at a time and store in an airtight container.

■ COOK'S TIP

Be careful not to overcook pasta. Drain it while it is al dente, which means it still has some bite to it. Never allow it to go soggy.

157 SAVOURY FRIED RICE

Preparation time:
10 minutes

Cooking time:
40 minutes

Serves 4

Calories:
261 per portion

Suitable for vegans

YOU WILL NEED:
salt
225 g/8 oz brown rice
1 tablespoon olive oil
100 g/4 oz frozen sweetcorn
6 spring onions, chopped
1 tablespoon soy sauce

Fill a large saucepan two-thirds full of water, add a teaspoonful of salt and bring to the boil. Add the rice, bring back to the boil and cook for about 30 minutes until the grains are tender, then drain. Heat the olive oil in another saucepan and add the rice, corn and spring onions, stirring all the time. Continue to stir-fry for 3-4 minutes, until all the ingredients are heated through. Add the soy sauce, and check seasoning before serving.

158 SPINACH LASAGNE

Preparation time:
20 minutes

Cooking time:
1 hour 15 minutes

Oven temperature:
190 C/375 F/gas 5

Serves 4

Calories:
578 per portion

YOU WILL NEED:
2 large onions, chopped
1 tablespoon olive oil
2 garlic cloves, crushed
2 × 400 g/14 oz can tomatoes
salt and pepper
450 g/1 lb packet frozen leaf spinach,
 thawed, or 900 g/2 lb fresh spinach,
 cooked, drained and chopped
350 g/12 oz vegetarian cream cheese
100 g/4 oz quick-cook lasagne
FOR THE TOPPING
soft wholewheat breadcrumbs
a little butter or margarine

Fry the onions in the oil for 5 minutes, then add the garlic and fry for a further 5 minutes, without browning. Purée 3 tablespoons of this onion mixture in a blender with the tomatoes and some salt and pepper to make a sauce. Add the rest of the onion to the spinach, together with the cream cheese and seasoning to taste. Put a layer of spinach mixture into the bottom of a shallow, ovenproof dish and cover with a layer of lasagne, then half the tomato sauce. Repeat the layers, ending with the sauce. Sprinkle crumbs all over the top of the lasagne and dot with butter or margarine. Bake, uncovered, for 50-60 minutes. If more convenient, this can cook for 1½-2 hours at a lower temperature, 150 C/300 F/gas 2.

■ COOK'S TIP

As a variation, stir in 50 g/ 2 oz beansprouts before serving. Alternatively, serve with Tofu with bamboo shoots and carrots (see recipe 107).

■ COOK'S TIP

This dish can be varied by adding more cheeses: 50 g/ 2 oz grated Parmesan can be added to the spinach mixture, and 175-225 g/ 6-8 oz Mozzarella can be *sliced and layered with the lasagne, spinach mixture and sauce, for a richer (more fattening!) version.*

159 TWO CHEESE LASAGNE

Preparation time:
20 minutes

Cooking time:
about 55 minutes

Oven temperature:
190 C/375 F/gas 5

Serves 4

Calories:
318 per portion

YOU WILL NEED:
300 ml/ ½ pint skimmed milk
1 small onion stuck with 4 cloves
20 g/ ¾ oz butter
20 g/ ¾ oz plain flour
salt and pepper
225 g/8 oz runner beans, sliced
*150 g/5 oz green or wholemeal quick-
 cook lasagne*
*225 g/8 oz vegetarian cottage cheese,
 sieved*
2 tablespoons chopped parsley
1 garlic clove, crushed
150 ml/ ¼ pint natural yogurt
1 egg
3 tablespoons grated Parmesan cheese

Put the milk into a pan with the onion. Bring to the boil and leave to stand, off the heat, for 15 minutes. Melt the butter in a pan and stir in the flour; cook for 1 minute. Gradually stir in the strained milk and cook until thickened. Season to taste.

Cook the beans, then drain and save the cooking liquid.

Put one-third of the lasagne into a greased ovenproof dish; thin the white sauce with a little of the bean cooking liquid, and spoon half over the lasagne. Top with the beans, and then with a second layer of lasagne. Mix the cottage cheese with the parsley and garlic, spread over the lasagne and top with the remaining sauce. Arrange the remaining lasagne on top. Beat the yogurt with the egg and Parmesan; spoon over the top of the lasagne. Bake in a preheated oven for about 45 minutes.

160 TOMATO TAGLIATELLE

Preparation time:
20 minutes

Cooking time:
25 minutes

Serves 4

Calories:
506 per portion

YOU WILL NEED:
450 g/1 lb fresh red tagliatelle
salt and pepper
2 tablespoons vegetable oil
15 g/ ½ oz soft margarine
2 medium onions, sliced
2 garlic cloves, crushed
450 g/1 lb courgettes, thinly sliced
1 green pepper, cored, seeded and sliced
2 large tomatoes, skinned and chopped
225 g/8 oz button mushrooms, sliced
2 tablespoons chopped fresh parsley
cheese topping (see Cook's Tip)
sprigs of oregano, to garnish

Cook the tagliatelle in lightly salted water for about 5 minutes, or until it is just tender (al dente). Drain the pasta, run hot water through it to prevent it from becoming sticky, and drain it again. Return to the pan and keep warm.

To make the sauce, heat the oil and margarine in a saucepan and fry the onions over moderate heat for 3 minutes, stirring once or twice. Add the garlic, courgettes and green pepper and fry for 3 minutes. Add the tomatoes and mushrooms, stir well, cover the pan and simmer for 10 minutes, or until the vegetables are just tender. Season with salt and pepper and stir in the parsley.

Turn the tagliatelle into a heated serving dish, pour on the sauce and toss. Spoon the cheese topping into the centre, garnish with sprigs of oregano and serve at once.

■ COOK'S TIP

Mild-tasting cottage cheese is made from skimmed milk curds which have been washed and rinsed. Being very low in fat, it is popular with slimmers.

■ COOK'S TIP

For the cheese topping: mix together 150 g/5 oz low-fat vegetarian cottage cheese (sieved), 25 g/1 oz vegetarian Cheddar cheese (grated), 2 tablespoons chopped *parsley and 2 tablespoons natural yogurt. Season to taste.*

161 PASTA WITH RICH TOMATO SAUCE

Preparation time:
25 minutes

Cooking time:
30 minutes

Serves 3-4

Calories:
391-293 per portion

Suitable for vegans using soya margarine

YOU WILL NEED:

25 g/1 oz butter or soya margarine
1 large onion, sliced
1 garlic clove, crushed
750 g/1½ lb ripe tomatoes, skinned and chopped
1 tablespoon tomato purée
2 teaspoons caster or granulated sugar
2 tablespoons fresh marjoram
150 ml/5 fl oz vegetable stock (recipe 3)
salt and pepper
250 g/9 oz wholewheat pasta shells
Crunchy dressing (see Cook's Tip)

Melt the butter or soya margarine in a pan and fry the onion and garlic for about 7 minutes until cooked but not brown. Add the tomatoes, tomato purée, sugar, marjoram, stock, salt and pepper. Half cover the pan and simmer gently for 25 minutes.

Remove the lid and cook a little faster for 2-3 minutes to reduce the sauce. It should have a thick, rich consistency. Keep the sauce hot.

Meanwhile, cook the pasta. Bring a large pan of salted water to the boil, add the pasta and cook for about 15 minutes, until just soft (al dente).

Drain the pasta thoroughly, turn into a warm serving dish, spoon the hot sauce over, and top with the crunchy dressing. Serve immediately.

■ COOK'S TIP

For the Crunchy dressing: brown 25 g/1 oz sunflower seeds in 10 g/¼ oz butter or soya margarine. Stir in 25 g/1 oz wholemeal breadcrumbs. Shake the pan over the heat until the breadcrumbs are also brown.

162 VEGETARIAN CHILLI WITH BROWN RICE

Preparation time:
20 minutes, plus soaking

Cooking time:
30 minutes (2 hours for dried beans)

Serves 4

Calories:
269 per portion

Suitable for vegans

YOU WILL NEED:

175 g/6 oz dried red kidney beans or
2 × 400 g/14 oz cans red kidney beans
1 onion, chopped
1 green pepper, seeded and chopped
1 tablespoon olive oil
1 garlic clove, crushed
400 g/14 oz can tomatoes
150 g/5 oz cooked green lentils (see recipe 163)
½-1 teaspoon chilli powder
1 teaspoon mild paprika
salt and pepper
sugar
225 g/8 oz brown rice, cooked (see recipe 155)

If using dried kidney beans, soak for 6-8 hours then drain; cover with fresh water, boil hard for 10 minutes, then simmer gently for 1¼-1½ hours, until tender.

Fry the onion and pepper in the oil in a large saucepan for 10 minutes, then add the garlic and tomatoes. Drain the red kidney beans and the lentils and add to the tomato mixture. Flavour with the paprika and chilli powder, salt, pepper and sugar to taste. Simmer for 10-15 minutes, season and serve with the brown rice.

■ COOK'S TIP

Always fast-boil kidney beans for at least 10 minutes of the cooking time to dispel harmful toxins, then lower the heat to a gentle boil.

163 SPAGHETTI WITH LENTIL BOLOGNESE SAUCE

Preparation time:
20 minutes, plus 40 minutes for lentils

Cooking time:
45 minutes

Serves 4

Calories:
604 per portion

Suitable for vegans using soya margarine

YOU WILL NEED:
225-350 g/8-12 oz spaghetti
½ oz butter or soya margarine
freshly ground black pepper
FOR THE SAUCE
225 g/8 oz cooked whole green lentils
   (see Cook's Tip)
2 onions, chopped
2 tablespoons oil
2 garlic cloves, crushed
2 celery sticks, chopped
2 carrots, finely diced
2 tablespoons tomato purée
salt and pepper

Prepare the sauce: drain the lentils, keeping the liquid. Fry the onions in the oil for 5 minutes, then add the garlic, celery and carrots. Simmer, covered, for 15 minutes, until tender. Stir in the lentils, tomato purée, seasoning and a little of the reserved liquid to make a thick, soft consistency. Simmer for about 10 minutes, adding more liquid if necessary. Half fill a large pan with water, add a teaspoonful of salt and bring to the boil. Add the spaghetti and simmer for about 10 minutes, until just tender. Drain the spaghetti, then return to the saucepan with the butter or soya margarine and pepper. Make sure the spaghetti is hot, then turn it on to a hot serving dish and pour the sauce on top. Hand round grated cheese separately (cheese not suitable for vegans).

■ COOK'S TIP

Green lentils do not need pre-soaking. Simply rinse, place in a pan, cover with water and bring to the boil. Simmer gently for about 40 minutes until tender.

164 SPICED BROWN RICE WITH BROCCOLI

Preparation time:
20 minutes

Cooking time:
30-40 minutes

Serves 2

Calories:
623 per portion

Suitable for vegans using soya margarine

YOU WILL NEED:
15 g/½ oz butter or soya margarine
1 medium onion, finely sliced
175 g/6 oz long-grain brown rice
450 ml/¾ pint vegetable stock (see
   recipe 3)
175 g/6 oz broccoli, trimmed
1 tablespoon olive oil
50 g/2 oz pine nuts
salt and pepper
½ teaspoon garam masala (optional)

Melt the butter or soya margarine and fry the onion until golden. Add the rice and fry gently for 2-3 minutes. Pour in the stock and bring to the boil, then cover the pan, lower the heat and simmer gently for 35-40 minutes until the rice is cooked but still slightly chewy, and all the stock has been absorbed.

About 15 minutes before the rice is cooked, prepare the broccoli. Cut the heads into thin strips lengthways, heat the olive oil in a large frying pan and stir-fry the broccoli for about 10 minutes. If you like the broccoli soft rather than slightly crisp, cover the pan for part of the time. This will create steam which will soften it further.

When the broccoli is cooked to taste add the pine nuts to the pan and stir-fry until they are lightly browned. Stir in the cooked rice, adding black pepper and a little salt if necessary. Spoon into a serving dish, sprinkle lightly with garam masala (if liked) and serve immediately.

■ COOK'S TIP

Although bright green broccoli looks attractive, several other vegetables could be used for this recipe: courgettes, mushrooms or peppers for instance.

165 SPAGHETTI WITH THREE HERBS SAUCE

Preparation time:
15 minutes

Cooking time:
about 12 minutes

Serves 4

Calories:
325 per portion

YOU WILL NEED:

3 tablespoons chopped fresh parsley
1 tablespoon chopped fresh tarragon
2 tablespoons chopped fresh basil
1 tablespoon olive oil
1 large garlic clove, crushed
4 tablespoons vegetable stock (see recipe 3)
2 tablespoons dry white wine
salt and pepper
350 g/12 oz wholewheat spaghetti

Put the parsley, tarragon, basil, olive oil, garlic, vegetable stock, white wine and salt and pepper to taste into a liquidizer and blend until smooth.

Cook the spaghetti in a large pan of boiling, salted water until just tender; test a strand from time to time, as wholewheat spaghetti takes longer to cook than the standard variety (about 12 minutes in total).

Drain the spaghetti and heap in a warmed bowl; pour over the herb sauce and toss well. Serve with a crisp salad.

166 PEPERONATA WITH WHOLEMEAL NOODLES

Preparation time:
20-25 minutes

Cooking time:
20 minutes

Serves 4

Calories:
315 per portion

YOU WILL NEED:

3 tablespoons olive oil
2 large onions, thinly sliced
1 large garlic clove, crushed
2 red peppers, seeded and cut into strips
2 green peppers, seeded and cut into strips
450 g/1 lb tomatoes, skinned, seeded and chopped
1 tablespoon chopped fresh basil
salt and pepper
175 g/6 oz wholewheat noodles
sprigs of fresh basil, to garnish

Heat 2 tablespoons olive oil in a deep frying pan. Add the onions and garlic and cook very gently until the onions soften. Add the peppers, tomatoes, basil and salt and pepper to taste. Cover and cook gently for 10 minutes. Remove the lid from the pan and cook over a fairly high heat until most of the moisture has evaporated. Keep warm.

Meanwhile, cook the noodles in plenty of boiling, salted water until just tender. Drain the noodles thoroughly and toss in the remaining olive oil; add salt and pepper to taste.

Divide the noodles among 4 serving plates and spoon the hot peperonata over the top. Garnish with sprigs of fresh basil and serve immediately as a light main course with a salad.

▓ COOK'S TIP

Don't just stick to spaghetti, there is a wide range of other pastas suited to this sauce. Try tubular rigatoni, curled fusilli, shells or the large bows called farfalle.

▓ COOK'S TIP

Peperonata is a classic summer dish, combining the best of the summer produce – peppers, fresh tomatoes and fresh basil. Use fresh wholemeal noodles if you *can find them; these will take about 8-10 minutes to cook.*

167 SPRING GREEN AND RICE MOULD

Preparation time: 20 minutes	YOU WILL NEED: 750 g/1½ lb spring greens
Cooking time: about 50 minutes	3 eggs 4 tablespoons natural yogurt 6 tablespoons cooked brown rice (see
Oven temperature: 180 C/350 F/gas 4	recipe 155) 50 g/2 oz grated Parmesan cheese
Serves 4	pinch of ground nutmeg salt and pepper
Calories: 173 per portion	1 tablespoon chopped chives FOR THE GARNISH watercress sprigs parsley sprigs

Wash the greens and shake dry; discard any tough stalk pieces. Shred the greens coarsely and put them into a pan with just enough boiling water to cover the base of the pan; cover and cook gently until they are just tender.

Drain the greens thoroughly, pressing to extract as much excess moisture as possible; blend to a purée.

Mix the purée with the remaining ingredients. Transfer to a greased 900 ml/1½ pint mould.

Stand the mould in a roasting tin and add sufficient hot water to come half-way up the sides; cover the top of the mould with a circle of lightly greased foil.

Bake in a preheated oven for 45 minutes, until the mould is set. Allow to stand for 2-3 minutes, then carefully turn out on to a plate. Garnish with watercress and parsley.

■ COOK'S TIP

A cheese mill, a cylindrical enclosed grater, is useful for Parmesan. The cheese is stored in it and the lid is turned to grate it straight on to the food.

168 MUNG BEAN AND FRESH HERB RISOTTO

Preparation time: 15 minutes, plus soaking	YOU WILL NEED: 175 g/6 oz mung beans, soaked for 2 hours in cold water
Cooking time: about 50 minutes	15 g/½ oz butter or soya margarine 1½ tablespoons vegetable oil 1 large onion, chopped
Serves 4	225 g/8 oz long-grain brown rice 750 ml/1¼ pints hot vegetable stock
Calories: 327 per portion	(see recipe 3) 3 tablespoons chopped mixed fresh
Suitable for vegans using soya margarine	herbs (parsley, thyme, basil, mint) salt and pepper 2 tablespoons pumpkin seeds

Drain and rinse the beans.

Using a large pan with a well-fitted lid, heat the butter or soya margarine and 1 tablespoon of the oil and fry the onion for 3 minutes, then stir in the beans and rice. Pour on the hot stock and bring to the boil. Cover the pan, lower the heat and simmer gently for 40 minutes until the beans and rice are tender and all the stock has been absorbed.

Add the herbs, salt and pepper and gently fork them through the mixture. Spoon the risotto into a warm serving dish and keep warm.

Fry the pumpkin seeds rapidly in the remaining oil for ½ minute (take care, as they jump about in the heat) then sprinkle over the risotto. Serve hot.

■ COOK'S TIP

Pumpkin seeds are dull green, oval shaped and flat. They come from fully matured ripe pumpkins and are widely available from health food shops. Rich in iron and vitamin C, they also contain a high amount of protein.

LIGHT MEALS

When time is short, use cheese and eggs with quick-cooking vegetables for an easy supper dish. Broccoli, cauliflower and courgettes all take less than 10 minutes to cook. Fill wholemeal bread or pittas with low-fat cheese, nuts or a salad for a healthy lunchtime snack, or choose one of the colourful salads included here.

169 POTATO JACKETS WITH SOURED CREAM DIP

Preparation time:
10 minutes

Cooking time:
1½-1¾ hours

Oven temperature:
190 C/375 F/gas 5

Serves 4

Calories:
306 per portion

YOU WILL NEED:
5 large potatoes, scrubbed and dried
150 ml/5 fl oz soured cream
1 teaspoon snipped fresh chives
salt and pepper
vegetable oil, for frying

Prick the potatoes with a fork and bake in a preheated oven for about 1¼ hours until tender.

Meanwhile, prepare the dip. Mix the soured cream with the chives and salt and pepper to taste. Spoon into a bowl, cover and leave in the refrigerator.

When the potatoes are cooked, leave to cool for a few minutes then cut each one lengthways into 4. Scoop out most of the potato, leaving just a thin layer next to the skin.

Pour vegetable oil into a small pan to a depth of 7.5 cm/ 3 inches. There is no need to use a large deep-frying pan.

Heat the oil to 180-190 C/350-375 F or until a cube of bread browns in 30 seconds.

Fry 4-5 potato skins at a time for about 2 minutes until brown and crisp. Lift from the oil with a slotted spoon and drain on kitchen paper. Keep the skins hot in the oven while the remaining skins are cooking. Serve with the chilled dip.

■ COOK'S TIP

These golden, crisp potato skins are an American speciality. Use the insides of the potatoes for Colcannon (recipe 181) or as topping for a vegetable pie.

170 VEGETABLE KEBABS

Preparation time:
30 minutes, plus marinating

Cooking time:
15 minutes

Serves 6

Calories:
129 per portion

Suitable for vegans using soya margarine

YOU WILL NEED:
36 small button mushrooms, wiped
1 aubergine, cut into chunks, sprinkled
    with salt, left for 30 minutes, then
    rinsed and drained
1 medium red or green sweet pepper,
    seeded and cut into strips
24 baby pickling onions or 2 onions,
    cut into chunks
6 small courgettes, cut into thick slices
FOR THE MARINADE
3 tablespoons Dijon mustard
3 garlic cloves, crushed
3 tablespoons dark brown sugar
3 tablespoons soy sauce
3 tablespoons olive oil
1½ teaspoons salt

Thread the vegetables on to 12 skewers. Next, mix together the marinade ingredients. Lay the skewers flat on a non-metal tray, polythene container, large plate or casserole. Spoon the marinade over them, turning the skewers to make sure that all the vegetables are coated with the mixture. Leave to marinate for at least 1 hour, basting occasionally. Cook the kebabs on the grid of a barbecue or under a hot grill for 10-15 minutes, until the vegetables are tender. Serve the kebabs on a bed of special rice (see Cook's Tip) with the remaining marinade served separately in a small jug.

■ COOK'S TIP

For special rice, put 300 g/ 10 oz brown rice and 50 g/ 2 oz wild rice in a pan together with 900 ml/ 1½ pints vegetable stock. Cook the rice for 40-45 minutes until tender. Add 25 g/1 oz butter or soya margarine, some chopped herbs and stir over a low heat until well coated. Season and serve.

171 WILD MUSHROOM FEUILLETE

Preparation time:
30 minutes

Cooking time:
15 minutes

Serves 4

Calories:
693 per portion

YOU WILL NEED:
350 g/12 oz flaky pastry (not
  containing animal fat)
FOR THE FILLING
15 g/½ oz butter or margarine
450 g/1 lb white button mushrooms,
  wiped and sliced
350 g/12 oz oyster mushrooms, sliced
300 ml/½ pint carton soured cream
300 ml/½ pint carton single cream
1 garlic clove, crushed
salt and pepper
lemon twists, to garnish

Roll out the pastry to a thickness of about 3 mm/⅛ inch and cut out 6 × 7.5 cm/3 inch circles and 6 × 5 cm/2 inch ones. Put the circles on a baking sheet and bake in a preheated oven for 10-12 minutes, until puffed up and golden brown. Meanwhile, melt the butter or margarine and fry the white mushrooms and oyster mushrooms for 5 minutes, until tender. Remove the mushrooms with a slotted spoon and boil the remaining liquid rapidly until reduced to 1 tablespoon. Add the mushrooms, soured and single cream, garlic and seasoning.

To serve, place a large pastry circle on a warmed plate, with a serving of the mushroom mixture. Cover with one of the smaller pastry circles. Garnish with a twist of lemon. Serve with fresh vegetables (see Cook's Tip).

172 CAULIFLOWER RAMEKINS

Preparation time:
20-25 minutes

Cooking time:
about 30 minutes

Oven temperature:
190 C/375 F/gas 5

Serves 4

Calories:
100 per portion

YOU WILL NEED:
1 small cauliflower
salt
3 tablespoons wholemeal breadcrumbs
2 tablespoons natural yogurt
1 tablespoon chopped fresh dill
2 eggs, separated
2 tablespoons grated Parmesan cheese
1 teaspoon Pesto sauce
freshly ground black pepper
sprigs of fresh dill, to garnish

Trim off the leaves and base stalk from the cauliflower (reserve and use for soup). Divide the cauliflower into florets and cook in boiling, salted water until just tender. Drain the cauliflower well and mash to a purée.

Put the purée into a pan and stir over a gentle heat for 1-2 minutes; this will allow some of the excess moisture to evaporate.

Mix the purée with the breadcrumbs, yogurt, dill, egg yolks, half the Parmesan cheese, Pesto sauce and salt and pepper to taste. Whisk the egg whites until stiff but not dry; fold lightly but thoroughly into the cauliflower mixture.

Spoon into 4 greased ramekin dishes then sprinkle with the remaining Parmesan cheese. Bake in a preheated oven for about 15-20 minutes, until puffed and lightly golden. Serve piping hot, garnished with fresh dill.

■ COOK'S TIP

Serve this dish with such vegetables as steamed or boiled baby new potatoes, broccoli florets, carrots cut into matchsticks and mangetout.

■ COOK'S TIP

Dill is an aromatic, sweet herb which has the useful property of having a calming effect on the stomach, helping to ease the pangs of indigestion.

173 BROCCOLI WITH EGG CREAM SAUCE

Preparation time:	YOU WILL NEED:
10 minutes	350-400 g/12-14 oz broccoli spears
	600 ml/1 pint boiling water
Cooking time:	salt
20 minutes	pinch of grated nutmeg
	FOR THE SAUCE
Serves 4	150 ml/¼ pint double cream
	2 egg yolks, beaten
Calories:	1 sprig of parsley, chopped
214 per portion	freshly ground white pepper

Remove the leaves from the broccoli and trim the spears. Place the broccoli spears in a pan with the water, a pinch of salt and the nutmeg. Bring to the boil, then lower the heat, cover and cook for about 8-10 minutes. Drain thoroughly, reserving 150 ml/¼ pint of the cooking liquid.

To make the sauce, place the reserved cooking liquid in a small pan, stir in the cream and bring to just below boiling point. Add the egg yolks, stirring constantly. Add the parsley and salt and pepper to taste.

Pour the egg cream sauce over the broccoli and leave to stand in a warm place for about 5 minutes before serving.

174 CAULIFLOWER CRUMBLE

Preparation time:	YOU WILL NEED:
20 minutes	1 cauliflower, broken into florets
	salt
Cooking time:	2 tablespoons oil
40 minutes	4 tablespoons wholemeal flour
	350 ml/12 fl oz milk
Oven temperature:	1 × 326 g/11 ½ oz can sweetcorn,
190 C/375 F/gas 5	drained
	2 tablespoons chopped parsley
Serves 4	100 g/4 oz matured vegetarian Cheddar
	cheese, grated
Calories:	FOR THE TOPPING
453 per portion	50 g/2 oz wholemeal flour
	25 g/1 oz margarine
	25 g/1 oz porridge
	25 g/1 oz chopped almonds

Cook the cauliflower in boiling salted water for 5 minutes. Drain, reserving the water.

Heat the oil in the same pan and stir in the flour. Remove from the heat, add the milk, stirring until blended. Add 150 ml/¼ pint of the reserved cooking liquid, bring to the boil and cook for 3 minutes, until thickened. Stir in the sweetcorn, parsley and half the cheese. Gently fold in the cauliflower and turn into a 1.5 litre/2½ pint ovenproof dish.

For the topping, place the flour in a bowl and rub in the margarine until the mixture resembles fine breadcrumbs. Add the oats, almonds and remaining cheese. Sprinkle over the vegetable mixture and bake in a preheated oven for 30 minutes, until golden brown and crisp.

■ COOK'S TIP

As a quick standby, frozen double cream is very useful. Available as sticks in packets, simply take out the number of sticks required and defrost before use.

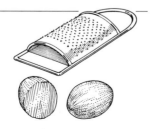

■ COOK'S TIP

Instead of using cauliflower, try a mixture of different vegetables. Carrots, green beans, broccoli, swede or parsnip all make interesting alternatives. Add some sesame seeds to the topping for extra protein.

175 STUFFED SPINACH LEAVES

Preparation time:
15 minutes

Cooking time:
55 minutes

Oven temperature:
190 C/375 F/gas 5

Serves 4

Calories:
111 per portion

YOU WILL NEED:
12 large spinach leaves, stalks removed
salt and pepper
1 tablespoon oil
1 onion, chopped
2 garlic cloves, crushed
225 g/8 oz mushrooms, chopped
75 g/3 oz wholemeal breadcrumbs
1 tablespoon chopped mixed herbs, e.g.
  parsley, thyme and marjoram
1 egg, beaten

Put the spinach in a large pan with 300 ml/½ pint salted water and boil for 2 minutes. Drain, reserving the liquid. Rinse and pat dry.

Heat the oil in a pan, add the onion and fry until softened. Add the garlic and mushrooms and cook for 5 minutes. Stir in the breadcrumbs, herbs, egg, and salt and pepper.

Place 1 tablespoon of the mixture in the centre of each spinach leaf, fold in both sides and roll up.

Lay the spinach rolls in a shallow ovenproof dish and pour over 150 ml/¼ pint of the reserved liquid. Cover with foil and bake in a preheated oven for 45 minutes. Lift out with a slotted spoon and reserve the juices. Serve with Lemon sauce (see Cook's Tip).

176 VEGETABLE CURRY

Preparation time:
30 minutes

Cooking time:
1 hour

Serves 4

Calories:
145 per portion

YOU WILL NEED:
2 tablespoons oil
1 onion, sliced
2 teaspoons ground coriander
2 teaspoons ground cumin
2 garlic cloves, crushed
5 cm/2 inch piece of fresh root ginger,
  chopped
1 × 397 g/14 oz can chopped tomatoes
1 green chilli, finely chopped
2 potatoes, diced
2 carrots, sliced
175 g/6 oz okra chopped
225 g/8 oz cauliflower, broken into
  florets
salt and pepper
2 tablespoons chopped fresh coriander

Heat the oil in a large pan, add the onion and fry until softened. Add the ground coriander, cumin, garlic and ginger and fry for 1 minute, stirring constantly. Add the tomatoes, 150 ml/¼ pint water, chilli, potatoes, carrots, okra, cauliflower and salt and pepper to taste. Mix to coat the vegetables with the sauce. Cover and cook gently for 20 minutes, until tender. Stir in the chopped coriander.

Serve the Vegetable curry on a bed of brown rice (see recipe 155) and with such typical curry accompaniments as Cucumber raita (see Cook's Tip).

■ COOK'S TIP

For Lemon sauce, whisk 2 egg yolks with 1 tablespoon lemon juice over a pan of simmering water. Add the reserved vegetable juices and stir for about 5 minutes until *thickened. Season and pour over the rolls.*

■ COOK'S TIP

For Cucumber raita, grate ¼ cucumber and drain off any juices. Mix with 150 g/ 5 oz natural yogurt and salt to taste. Sprinkle with paprika before serving.

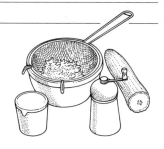

177 POPOVERS

Preparation time:
25 minutes

Cooking time:
25 minutes

Oven temperature:
220 C/425 F/gas 8

Serves 4-6

Calories:
246-164 per portion

YOU WILL NEED:
1 tablespoon vegetable oil
1 large onion, thinly sliced
450 g/1 lb ripe tomatoes, skinned and
  chopped
1 teaspoon soy sauce
2 teaspoons tomato purée
salt and pepper
FOR THE BATTER
50 g/2 oz plain wholemeal flour
50 g/2 oz plain white flour
pinch of cayenne pepper
1 teaspoon dried mixed herbs
2 eggs, beaten
1 tablespoon vegetable oil, plus extra
150 ml/5 fl oz milk
150 ml/5 fl oz water

Heat the oil in a pan and fry the onion for 10 minutes until brown. Add the tomatoes, soy sauce, tomato purée, salt and plenty of pepper. Bring to simmering point, stirring, then cover the pan and cook gently for 10 minutes.

Make the batter. Put the flours, ½ teaspoon salt, pepper, cayenne and herbs into a bowl. Add the eggs, oil and half the milk and mix to a smooth paste. Gradually whisk in the remaining milk and the water. Pour the batter into a jug.

Oil 2 trays of 12 tart tins and put them in a preheated oven until smoking hot. Remove from the oven, pour the batter into the tins, almost filling them, and bake for about 12 minutes until puffed up and golden. Serve with the hot sauce.

■ COOK'S TIP

The sauce can be prepared up to 24 hours in advance and kept tightly covered with clingfilm in the refrigerator. Reheat when the popovers are ready to come out of the oven. The batter can be made up to 8 hours in advance and kept in the refrigerator.

178 CURRIED SWEETCORN AND POTATO FRITTERS

Preparation time:
25 minutes

Cooking time:
25 minutes

Oven temperature:
110 C/250 F/gas ¼

Serves 4

Calories:
288 per portion

YOU WILL NEED:
50 g/2 oz plain wholemeal flour
salt and pepper
1 egg, lightly beaten
4 tablespoons milk
1 teaspoon hot curry paste
450 g/1 lb potatoes, unpeeled, washed
  and coarsely grated
1 medium onion, peeled and grated
1 × 200 g/7 oz can sweetcorn, drained
4-6 tablespoons vegetable oil, for frying

Put the flour, salt, pepper, egg, milk and curry paste into a large bowl and mix to a smooth, thick batter.

Put the grated potato into a clean cloth and twist both ends towards the middle to squeeze out any surplus, starchy liquid. Pat the potato dry with absorbent kitchen paper and add to the batter with the onion and sweetcorn.

Heat 1 tablespoon of the oil in a large frying pan and drop the mixture in 1 tablespoon at a time, gently nudging each fritter into a round flat shape with a fish slice. Cook about 4 fritters at a time.

Fry the fritters for 3-4 minutes on each side, then drain on kitchen paper and keep hot while frying the next batch.

Arrange the fritters on a warm dish and serve with a bowl of Yogurt and watercress dressing (see Cook's Tip).

■ COOK'S TIP

For Yogurt and watercress dressing, mix 150 ml/5 fl oz natural yogurt, seasoning and 1 bunch of finely chopped watercress. Let sit at room temperature 1 hour.

179 EGGS IN THE NEST

Preparation time:
15 minutes

Cooking time:
40 minutes

Oven temperature:
190 C/375 F/gas 5

Serves 4

Calories:
185 per portion

YOU WILL NEED:
350 g/12 oz potatoes, peeled
225 g/8 oz parsnips, peeled and sliced
salt
25 g/1 oz soft margarine
5 eggs
freshly ground black pepper
pinch of grated nutmeg
2 tablespoons chopped fresh parsley
75 g/3 oz low-fat vegetarian Cheddar
  cheese, grated
sprigs of parsley, to garnish

Cook the potatoes and parsnips in boiling, salted water for 15-20 minutes until they are tender. Drain and mash. Beat in the margarine and 1 of the eggs and season with salt, pepper and nutmeg. Stir in the parsley and 40 g/1½ oz of the cheese.

Spoon the potato mixture into four 10 cm/4 inch greased individual baking rings standing on a baking sheet, or muffin tins, and shape it to make nests. Make a ridge round the top with a fork. Break 1 egg into each 'nest' and sprinkle the remaining cheese on top.

Bake in a preheated oven for 15-20 minutes until the eggs are set. Garnish with the parsley and serve at once.

180 STUFFED VINE LEAVES

Preparation time:
45 minutes, plus cooling

Cooking time:
1½ hours

Serves 4

Calories:
240 per portion

Suitable for vegans

YOU WILL NEED:
225 g/8 oz preserved vine leaves,
  drained (see Cook's Tip)
175 g/6 oz brown rice
1 small onion, finely chopped
2 tablespoons chopped fresh parsley
2 tablespoons chopped fresh mint
generous pinch of ground cinnamon
generous pinch of mixed spice
2 garlic cloves, crushed
50 g/2 oz pine nuts, chopped
50 g/2 oz currants
finely grated zest of ½ lemon
salt and pepper
250 ml/8 fl oz water

Soak the brown rice in boiling water for 2-3 minutes, then rinse under cold water, drain and mix with the onion, parsley, mint, spices, garlic, pine nuts, currants, lemon zest and salt and pepper to taste.

Use a few damaged or mis-shapen vine leaves to line the base and sides of a large frying pan; reserve 4-6 perfect leaves for serving. Divide the rice mixture among the remaining leaves; fold in the edges and roll up the leaves, so that the filling is completely enclosed. Pack the stuffed leaves closely together in the lined pan. Pour over the water. Cover the pan tightly, and simmer very gently for 1½ hours; top up with more water if the liquid evaporates too much during cooking.

Allow to cool in the pan. Place a perfect vine leaf on each serving plate, and arrange 5-6 stuffed leaves on top.

■ COOK'S TIP

Eggs are an important source of protein and iron, but are also high in saturated fat. Two or three a week is the nutritional recommendation.

■ COOK'S TIP

Put the vine leaves into a bowl and cover with boiling water. Stir the leaves so that they separate. Drain the leaves separately on absorbent paper.

181 COLCANNON

Preparation time:
15 minutes

Cooking time:
40 minutes

Oven temperature:
200 C/400 F/gas 6

Serves 4

Calories:
142 per portion

YOU WILL NEED:
225 g/8 oz shredded white cabbage
salt
600 g/1 ¼ lb potatoes, cooked and
    mashed without milk or butter
25 g/1 oz butter
1 medium onion, chopped
freshly ground black pepper
2 teaspoons poppy seeds

Cook the cabbage in a little boiling, salted water for about 6 minutes until crisply tender. Drain and put into a bowl with the mashed potato.

Meanwhile, melt half the butter in a small pan and gently fry the onion until golden. Stir into the cabbage and potato and add a little salt and plenty of black pepper.

Use the remaining 15 g/½ oz butter to grease a 450 g/1 lb loaf tin, and scatter the poppy seeds over the base and sides of the tin to coat.

Spoon the cabbage and potato mixture into the tin, smooth the top and cover with foil. Bake in a preheated oven for 40 minutes, then turn out on to a hot dish and serve immediately.

182 STUFFED AVOCADO SALAD

Preparation time:
20 minutes

Serves 2

Calories:
341 per portion

YOU WILL NEED:
1 large ripe avocado, halved and stoned
1 tablespoon lemon juice
2 tomatoes, skinned and chopped
2 spring onions, chopped
½ small green pepper, seeded and finely
    chopped
50 g/2 oz vegetarian Cheddar cheese,
    grated
salt and pepper
4 lettuce leaves
few sprigs watercress
1 carrot, scraped and cut into
    matchsticks

Using a teaspoon, scoop out the avocado flesh, being careful not to damage the skin which will be needed for serving the salad. Dice the flesh and place in a bowl with the lemon juice, tomatoes, spring onions, green pepper and cheese. Season to taste. Spoon the mixture into the avocado skins. Arrange the stuffed avocados on the lettuce leaves and garnish with watercress and carrot sticks.

■ COOK'S TIP

This dish, which can be served with Two-bean vegetable goulash (see recipe 47), Tomato sauce (see recipe 52) or just on its own, is an excellent way of using *the insides of the potatoes left from the Potato jackets (see recipe 169).*

■ COOK'S TIP

Cover the avocado with the lemon juice as soon as possible after cutting to prevent discoloration. If the salad has to sit a while, cover the dishes with clingfilm.

183 DEEP-DISH SALAD BOWL

Preparation time:
30 minutes

Serves 2

Calories:
211 per portion

YOU WILL NEED:
4 lettuce leaves, shredded
100 g/4 oz cold cooked potato, diced
4 tablespoons mayonnaise or soured
  cream, or a mixture of both
salt and pepper
100 g/4 oz beansprouts (see Cook's
  Tip)
1 tablespoon olive oil
1 tablespoon wine vinegar
2 tomatoes, chopped
10 cm/4 inch piece cucumber, cubed
2 tablespoons raisins
1 large carrot, finely grated
1 raw beetroot, peeled and finely grated
salad cress or watercress, to garnish

Put the shredded lettuce in the bottom of two deep dishes or soup bowls. Mix the potato with half the mayonnaise, soured cream or mixture; season, then spoon into the bowls. Mix the beansprouts with oil, vinegar and some salt and pepper to taste. Put these on top of the potatoes, followed by the tomatoes, cucumber, raisins, grated carrot and beetroot. Spoon the remaining mayonnaise, soured cream or mixture on top of the beetroot and sprinkle with some salad cress or watercress. Serve immediately.

184 COURGETTE FRITTERS

Preparation time:
30 minutes

Cooking time:
20 minutes

Oven temperature:
110 C/225 F/gas ¼

Serves 4

Calories:
248 per portion

YOU WILL NEED:
5 small courgettes, about 275 g/10 oz
FOR THE BATTER
100 g/4 oz wholemeal self-raising flour
salt and pepper
1 egg
1 tablespoon vegetable oil
2 teaspoons vinegar
150 ml/5 fl oz milk
vegetable oil, for frying
Stilton dip (see Cook's Tip)

Trim the courgettes and cut into short sticks about 5 cm/ 2 inches long and 5 mm/¼ inch wide. Dry on kitchen paper.

Make the batter. Put the flour, salt, pepper, egg, oil, vinegar and half the milk into a basin, whisk to a thick paste then gradually whisk in the rest of the milk.

Pour the vegetable oil into a small pan to a depth of about 7.5 cm/3 inches; there is no need to use a large deep frying pan. Heat the oil to 180-190 C/350-375 F or until a cube of bread browns in 30 seconds.

Dip each piece of courgette into the batter, allowing any excess to run back into the bowl, and then fry in small batches until puffy and golden (about 3 minutes per batch). Lift out with a slotted spoon, drain on absorbent kitchen paper, and keep hot on a serving dish in the preheated oven until you have completed the frying.

Sprinkle the fritters lightly with salt and serve hot with the Stilton dip.

■ COOK'S TIP

To sprout beans, select clean, whole seeds of any variety except kidney beans. Soak in cold water, drain and place in a large glass jar. Cover with muslin, securing with a *rubber band. Twice a day, pour cold water through the muslin, then drain off. The seeds should sprout in 4-5 days.*

■ COOK'S TIP

For the Stilton dip: mix 4 tablespoons mayonnaise and 4 tablespoons natural yogurt. Fold in 50 g/2 oz crumbled vegetarian Stilton. Season with pepper.

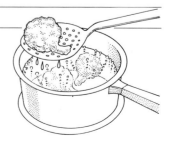

185 COLOURFUL BEETROOT SALAD

Preparation time:
30 minutes

Cooking time:
1¼-1½ hours

Serves 4

Calories:
251 per portion

YOU WILL NEED:
600-750 g/1¼-1½ lb beetroot
salt
1 fennel bulb, cut into julienne strips
1 apple, cored and chopped
1 onion, sliced into rings
1 × 150 g/5 oz carton natural yogurt
4 tablespoons double cream
1 teaspoon creamed horseradish
pinch of sugar
1 tablespoon chopped hazelnuts
1-2 hard-boiled eggs, shelled
sprigs of fennel, to garnish

Scrub the beetroot under running water. Place the beetroot in a large saucepan and cover with boiling water. Add a pinch of salt and bring back to the boil. Lower the heat and cook gently for about 1½ hours until tender.

Rinse the beetroot under cold water and leave to cool slightly. Peel, then slice, thinly. Place in a large serving bowl. Add the fennel, apple and onion and toss well to mix.

To make the dressing, beat the yogurt with the cream, horseradish, sugar and hazelnuts. Pour over the beetroot salad and toss well to mix.

Cut the hard-boiled egg into quarters and arrange on top of the salad. Garnish with fennel sprigs if liked.

▧ COOK'S TIP

For a quicker recipe, buy ready-cooked beetroot. Choose ones that haven't been cooked with vinegar as they are too sharp for this dish.

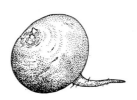

186 HEALTH CLUB SANDWICHES

Preparation time:
25 minutes

Serves 4

Calories:
250 per fruity sandwich
210 per vegetable sandwich

YOU WILL NEED:
8 slices rye or wholewheat bread
175 g/6 oz low-fat soft vegetarian cheese
75 g/3 oz currants
1 teaspoon grated lemon zest
50 g/2 oz dried, stoned dates, chopped
2 dessert apples, peeled, cored, sliced
1 tablespoon lemon juice
1 kiwi fruit, peeled and sliced
4 mint sprigs, to garnish
150 g/5 oz cottage cheese, sieved
25 g/1 oz vegetarian Cheddar, grated
2 tablespoons snipped fresh chives
salt and pepper
2 medium carrots, grated
50 g/2 oz button mushrooms, sliced
1 tablespoon French dressing
2 hard-boiled eggs, sliced

Cut the crusts from the bread. Beat the soft cheese and stir in the currants, lemon zest and dates. Spread 4 of the bread slices with this mixture. Toss the apple slices in the lemon juice, then arrange them on the sandwich base, followed by the kiwi fruit. Garnish with mint sprigs.

Beat the sieved cottage cheese, then beat in the grated cheese and chives, season and spread over the remaining 4 bread slices. Sprinkle the grated carrot over and press it lightly into the cheese. Toss the mushroom slices in the dressing and arrange them and the egg slices over the carrot topping.

▧ COOK'S TIP

Add chopped walnuts or hazelnuts to the low-fat soft cheese for a delicious crunch. Try using vegetarian Stilton instead of Cheddar for the vegetable sandwich.

187 NUTBURGERS IN SOFT BAPS

Preparation time:
20 minutes

Cooking time:
25 minutes

Serves 4

Calories:
895 per portion

**Suitable for vegans
using soya margarine**

YOU WILL NEED:
2 onions, chopped
2 celery sticks, finely diced
100 g/4 oz butter or soya margarine
2 teaspoons dried mixed herbs
2 tablespoons wholewheat flour
300 ml/ ½ pint vegetable stock (see
    recipe 3)
2 tablespoons soy sauce
2 teaspoons yeast extract
450 g/1 lb mixed nuts: almonds, Brazil
    nuts, walnuts, cashew nuts, finely
    chopped
225 g/8 oz soft wholewheat
    breadcrumbs
salt and pepper
dried breadcrumbs, to coat (see Cook's
    Tip)
olive oil for shallow frying

Fry the onions and celery in the butter or soya margarine for 10 minutes, browning them lightly. Add the herbs, stir for 1 minute, then mix in the flour and cook for a further 1-2 minutes. Pour in the vegetable stock and stir until thickened. Add the soy sauce, yeast extract, nuts, breadcrumbs and salt and pepper to taste. Allow the mixture to cool, then form into 12 flat burgers about 1 cm/½ inch thick, and coat with dry breadcrumbs. Cook on a flat, oiled tin (or frying pan) over the barbecue for 5 minutes each side. Serve in soft burger baps, with chutney and pickles as required.

188 RADICCHIO SALAD SUPREME

Preparation time:
30 minutes

Serves 4

Calories:
199 per portion

YOU WILL NEED:
1 radicchio
3-4 medium tomatoes, cut into wedges
100 g/4 oz vegetarian Camembert
    cheese, cubed
1 teaspoon made mustard
120 ml/4 fl oz whipping cream
salt and pepper
3 teaspoons chopped parsley
½ onion, chopped

Remove the outer leaves from the radicchio and keep to one side for garnish. Separate the heart, tearing larger leaves into pieces. Place in a sieve, rinse and drain thoroughly. Place in a mixing bowl. Add the tomatoes and cheese and mix well.

To make the dressing, beat the mustard with the cream, salt and pepper to taste, and 2 teaspoons parsley. Fold in the onion and pour over the salad. Toss lightly and leave to stand for a few minutes to allow the flavours to develop.

Line a salad bowl with the reserved radicchio leaves and fill with the salad. Sprinkle with the remaining parsley.

■ COOK'S TIP

Dried breadcrumbs are best for coating food before frying. Make fresh crumbs and let them dry out in a very cool oven until crisp. Keep in an airtight container.

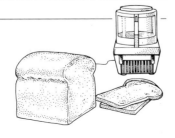

■ COOK'S TIP

Radicchio is an attractive, red, crinkly vegetable. Its slightly bitter leaves make an excellent, although expensive, salad ingredient. Radicchio is a good source of vitamin C.

189 BLINIS

Preparation time:
10 minutes, plus
standing

Cooking time:
20 minutes

Serves 6

Calories:
180 per portion

YOU WILL NEED:
100 g/4 oz buckwheat or plain
    wholemeal flour
100 g/4 oz plain white flour
½ teaspoon salt
2 teaspoons Easy Bake yeast
1 egg, separated
1 tablespoon vegetable oil
300 ml/ ½ pint tepid milk
a selection of toppings (see Cook's Tip)
sprigs of watercress, to garnish
    (optional)

Put the flours, salt, yeast, egg yolk and oil into a bowl. Pour in the tepid milk and mix to a thick smooth batter. Cover and leave to stand for 1 hour. The surface of the batter should be puffy and covered with bubbles.

Whisk the egg white and fold into the batter. The mixture is now ready for use.

Heat a lightly oiled griddle or frying pan over a steady heat. Drop 2 tablespoons of batter into the pan and cook for 3 minutes until tiny holes appear over the surface. Turn the pancake and cook the other side for 2 minutes. Cook 3-4 blinis at a time. When ready put them between the layers of a clean tea-towel, folded on a plate over a pan of boiling water. There should be 16-20.

To serve, arrange 2-3 warm blinis with one or more of the chosen toppings on a small plate and garnish with sprigs of watercress if liked.

190 WHEAT-FILLED PITTAS

Preparation time:
20 minutes, plus
soaking

Cooking time:
1¼ hours

Serves 4

Calories:
333 per portion

Suitable for vegans

YOU WILL NEED:
225 g/8 oz wholewheat grains, covered
    with cold water and soaked for 6-8
    hours or overnight
2 tablespoons red wine vinegar
2 tablespoons olive oil
1 medium onion, purple if possible,
    sliced
2 tablespoons chopped fresh parsley or
    chopped fresh coriander
2 tomatoes, skinned and chopped
salt and pepper
1 head radicchio or a small lettuce,
    separated into leaves
wholewheat pitta bread
watercress sprigs, flat leafed parsley or
    salad cress, to garnish

Drain the wheat, then put it into a saucepan and cover with fresh water. Bring to the boil and simmer for 1¼ hours, or 25 minutes in a pressure cooker. Drain and cool. Put the red wine vinegar into a bowl with the olive oil and add the wheat, onion, parsley, tomatoes and a little salt and pepper to taste. Spoon the mixture with the radicchio or lettuce leaves into warm wholewheat pitta bread. Garnish with watercress sprigs.

■ COOK'S TIP

Suggested toppings: cottage cheese with radish and cress; soured cream with chopped pecan nuts; mozzarella with stuffed olives; sliced tomatoes with soured cream.

■ COOK'S TIP

These hearty sandwiches make a delicious main course. Other fillings: endive and sliced tomatoes, cucumber and salad cress or thinly sliced courgettes and
watercress. If wholewheat pitta bread is unobtainable, split and fill large wholewheat baps.

191 CREAM CHEESE TOASTS

Preparation time:
10 minutes

Serves 6

Calories:
389 per portion

YOU WILL NEED:
175 g/6 oz vegetarian cream cheese
1 small beetroot, cooked or uncooked
1 tablespoon finely chopped parsley
2 hard-boiled egg yolks
pinch of turmeric
1 packet of Melba toasts
   (about 30 pieces), or see recipe 18
FOR THE GARNISHES
shelled pistachio nuts
salted cashew nuts
mashed hard-boiled egg yolk
little sprigs of parsley

Divide the cream cheese into three equal portions and put into separate bowls. Add a very little mashed or finely grated beetroot to one bowl; then beat the chopped parsley into another portion and finally mash the egg yolk until it is smooth and stir this into the third portion of cream cheese, together with the turmeric. Pipe or spread these mixtures on the Melba toasts. Top each with a pistachio nut, cashew nut, fresh parsley or other garnish as desired.

192 JACKET POTATOES WITH PESTO

Preparation time:
15-20 minutes

Cooking time:
1½ hours

Oven temperature:
190 C/375 F/gas 5

Serves 4

Calories:
320 per portion

YOU WILL NEED:
4 medium baking potatoes, about
   200 g/7 oz each
40 g/1 ½ oz butter
2 teaspoons Pesto sauce
salt and pepper
generous pinch of ground nutmeg
4 tablespoons chopped cooked spinach

Scrub the potatoes and dry them with absorbent kitchen paper. Prick each one several times with a fine skewer. Wrap each potato in foil, put into a preheated oven and bake for 1 hour 20 minutes, or until cooked.

Melt the butter; stir in the Pesto sauce and salt, pepper and nutmeg to taste.

Remove the potatoes from the oven and cut a thin horizontal slice from the top of each one. Fluff up the potato and make a slight well in the centre.

Spoon in a little of the Pesto butter, and then a spoonful of spinach. Top with the remaining Pesto-flavoured butter. Pull up the foil over each filled potato and return to the oven for a further 10 minutes.

Serve piping hot as a complete light meal.

■ COOK'S TIP

Watching the calories? Use a low-fat curd or cream cheese instead and go easy on the nuts to garnish. Although high in protein, they are also high in fat.

■ COOK'S TIP

Instead of pesto butter, stir in some garlic and herb cream cheese or grated vegetarian Cheddar. Serve with a large, fresh salad for a filling lunch or supper snack.

DESSERTS

Dessert is the great finale to any meal. Always plan what to make according to the fresh fruit in season and the preceding courses. Choose a rich, creamy or filling dessert such as Plum cheesecake, Fruit and nut crumble, or Chocolate roulade after a light meal. Tropical fruits in sherry, Strawberries with Cointreau or Hot spiced peaches would make a refreshing end to meals with more substantial main courses.

193 FROZEN BUTTERSCOTCH MOUSSE

Preparation time:
20 minutes, plus freezing

Cooking time:
20 minutes

Serves 6

Calories:
323 per portion

YOU WILL NEED:
100 g/4 oz light soft brown sugar
25 g/1 oz butter
pinch of salt
120 ml/4 fl oz water
4 egg yolks
250 ml/8 fl oz double cream
1 ½ teaspoons vanilla essence

Put the sugar, butter and salt in a saucepan. Stir until the sugar has dissolved and the butter melted, then bring to the boil. Boil for 1 minute. Stir in the water and cook until the butterscotch mixture is smooth and syrupy.

Beat the egg yolks in a heatproof bowl. Gradually beat in the butterscotch syrup. Place the bowl over a pan of simmering water and heat, beating, until the mixture is light and fluffy. Set aside to cool.

Whip the cream with the vanilla essence until thick. Fold into the butterscotch mixture. Pour into a decorative freezer-proof mould and freeze until firm.

Transfer the mousse to the refrigerator 30 minutes before serving. Serve with fresh soft fruit such as kiwi fruit and strawberries.

194 HOT SPICED PEACHES

Preparation time:
5 minutes

Cooking time:
15-20 minutes

Oven temperature:
180 C/350 F/gas 4

Serves 4

Calories:
112 per portion

YOU WILL NEED:
4 large ripe fresh peaches
grated zest of 1 lemon
¼ teaspoon ground cinnamon
2 tablespoons clear honey
15 g/½ oz butter

First skin the peaches. Dip them one at a time in boiling water and the skins will slide off very easily. Cut each peach in half and twist to separate the halves, then remove the stone.

Arrange the peach halves cut side up in an ovenproof dish. Sprinkle with the lemon zest and cinnamon then spoon the honey over.

Place a dot of butter in the cavity of each peach, cover the dish and bake for about 20 minutes until the peaches are tender and juicy.

■ COOK'S TIP

To turn the mousse out of its mould, dip the mould quickly into hot water and invert it on to a serving plate; the mousse should slide out without difficulty.

■ COOK'S TIP

A delightful late summer pudding. Serve the peaches hot from the oven with cream. If peaches are unavailable, look for fresh nectarines instead.

195 STRAWBERRIES WITH BLACKCURRANT SAUCE

Preparation time:
25 minutes, plus cooling

Cooking time:
5 minutes

Serves 4

Calories:
75 per portion

YOU WILL NEED:
225 g/8 oz fresh blackcurrants, strigs removed
2 tablespoons honey
3 tablespoons red wine
350 g/12 oz ripe strawberries, hulled and halved
small sprigs of fresh redcurrants, to decorate

Put the trimmed blackcurrants into a pan with the honey and red wine; stir well then simmer gently until the natural fruit juices are released (about 5 minutes).

Blend the lightly cooked blackcurrants and their liquid in a liquidizer until fairly smooth – the sauce should still have some texture. Allow to cool.

Arrange the halved strawberries in small decorative dishes and spoon the blackcurrant sauce near to them. Decorate with clusters of fresh redcurrants.

196 CHERRY COBBLER

Preparation time:
25 minutes

Cooking time:
50 minutes

Oven temperature:
200 C/400 F/gas 6

Serves 6

Calories:
320 per portion

YOU WILL NEED:
2 tablespoons orange juice
40 g/1 ½ oz light muscovado sugar
1 bay leaf
900 g/2 lb dessert cherries, stoned
FOR THE COBBLER DOUGH
225 g/8 oz wholewheat self-raising flour
1 teaspoon baking powder
salt
pinch of grated nutmeg
50 g/2 oz soft margarine
40 g/1 ½ oz demerara sugar
1 teaspoon grated orange zest
2 tablespoons orange juice
1 egg, beaten
100 ml/3 ½ fl oz natural yogurt

Put the orange juice, sugar and bay leaf into a frying pan and stir over low heat until the sugar has dissolved. Add the cherries, reserving a few for decoration, and simmer for about 10 minutes, shaking the pan frequently, until they are just tender. Turn the cherries into a baking dish and discard the bay leaf.

Make the cobbler dough (see Cook's Tip).

Roll out the dough on a lightly floured board until it is 2 cm/¾ inch thick. Use a heart-shaped biscuit cutter to cut out the dough. Arrange the scone shapes over the fruit, brush with milk and sprinkle on a little sugar.

Bake the pudding in a preheated oven for 35 minutes or until the topping is well risen and golden brown. Serve hot.

■ COOK'S TIP

This is an ideal dessert for slimmers and is rich in vitamin C. For a treat, try serving it with a scoop of Strawberry and yogurt ice (see recipe 213).

■ COOK'S TIP

For the cobbler dough, mix the dry ingredients together, rub in the margarine, stir in the sugar and grated orange zest, then the orange juice, egg and yogurt. Shape the *mixture into a ball in the mixing bowl and knead lightly.*

197 STRAWBERRIES WITH COINTREAU

Preparation time:
10 minutes, plus
macerating

Serves 4

Calories:
121 per portion

YOU WILL NEED:
*750 g/1 ½ lb small ripe strawberries,
 hulled and washed*
2-3 tablespoons fruit sugar
*3 tablespoons Cointreau or other
 orange liqueur*
*thin strips of zest from 1 large, well-
 scrubbed orange*

Put the strawberries into a bowl and sprinkle with the fruit sugar and Cointreau. Add the orange zest, stir gently, then cover and leave to macerate for 1 hour. Serve on individual plates, with the macerating liquid spooned over the strawberries.

198 GREEN FRUIT PUDDING

Preparation time:
25 minutes, plus
chilling

Cooking time:
20 minutes

Serves 6

Calories:
190 per portion

YOU WILL NEED:
*10 large slices wholewheat bread, crusts
 removed*
4-5 tablespoons clear honey
*350 g/12 oz gooseberries, topped and
 tailed*
*350 g/12 oz greengages, stoned and
 roughly chopped*
*2 small cooking apples, peeled, cored
 and thinly sliced*
*few mint or scented geranium leaves, to
 decorate*

Line a greased 1.2 litre/2 pint bowl or pudding basin with bread, cutting and fitting it to ensure there are no gaps.

Melt the honey in a large frying pan over low heat. Add all the fruit, reserving a few gooseberries for decoration. Shake the pan and simmer gently for about 12-15 minutes, until the fruit is quite tender.

Spoon a little of the juice over the bread, then pour in the fruit to fill the lined bowl. Cover the top with the remaining bread, taking great care to fit it closely and neatly around the rim. Cover the bowl with a saucer that just fits inside the rim, then weigh it down with a large filled can or something equally large and heavy.

Chill the pudding overnight. Run a knife around the edge and unmould it on to a flat serving plate. Decorate the pudding with the reserved gooseberries and leaves and serve it cold, cut into wedges, with chilled Greek yogurt.

■ COOK'S TIP

*Serve this dessert with
Strawberry yogurt ice (see
recipe 213), Greek yogurt or
some thin shortbread
biscuits.*

■ COOK'S TIP

*This is an autumn version of
a traditional summer
pudding. For this use
strawberries, raspberries,
redcurrants and
blackcurrants.*

199 BANANAS FLAMBE

Preparation time:
7-8 minutes

Serves 4

Calories:
295 per portion

YOU WILL NEED:
4 medium bananas, peeled and cut in
  half lengthways
50 g/2 oz butter, melted
50 g/2 oz light brown sugar
4 tablespoons brandy
flaked almonds, toasted, to decorate

Fry the bananas in the melted butter until they are golden and just tender.

Sprinkle in the sugar and stir carefully to coat the fruit. Stir in the brandy. Bring to the boil. Immediately set alight and, once the flames have died, serve sprinkled with a few flaked almonds.

200 GRAPE CHEESECAKE

Preparation time:
20 minutes

Cooking time:
1½ hours

Oven temperature:
160 C/325 F/gas 3

Serves 6

Calories:
555 per portion

YOU WILL NEED:
175 g/6 oz wholewheat biscuits,
  crushed
75 g/3 oz butter or margarine, melted
450 g/1 lb curd or cream cheese
150 ml/5 fl oz natural yogurt
4 tablespoons clear honey
50 g/2 oz Demerara sugar
4 eggs
2 tablespoons ground almonds
1 teaspoon vanilla extract or essence
FOR THE TOPPING
150 ml/¼ pint soured cream
100 g/4 oz each black and green grapes,
  halved and seeded
3 tablespoons clear honey

For the crust, mix together the biscuit crumbs and melted butter or margarine. Spoon into the bottom of a 20 cm/8 inch loose-bottom or spring-clip flan tin. Press down firmly.

Next, put the filling ingredients into a bowl and beat together until smooth and creamy. Pour on to the crumb crust and spread evenly. Bake the cheesecake in a preheated oven for 1-1¼ hours until firm in the centre. Remove the cheesecake from the oven and carefully spoon the soured cream on top, gently levelling it with a knife. Turn off the heat but put the cheesecake back in the still-warm oven for 15-20 minutes.

When cold, lift the cheesecake out of the tin. Arrange the grapes on top. Put the honey into a small saucepan and heat, then spoon or brush it over the grapes. Cool.

■ COOK'S TIP

Use a frying pan, not a deep-sided pan to flambé the fruit. It will be easier – and safer – to set the brandy alight from the side of the pan, not over the top.

■ COOK'S TIP

If a loose-bottomed tin is not available, grease and line a 20 cm/8 inch deep cake tin and place double thickness foil strips in a cross to lift out the cheesecake when set.

201 TROPICAL FRUITS IN SHERRY

Preparation time:
10 minutes, plus marinating

Serves 4

Calories:
118 per portion

Suitable for vegans

YOU WILL NEED:
1 medium-sized papaya (pawpaw)
2 kiwi fruit
2 small bananas
1 tablespoon lemon juice
150 ml/5 fl oz medium or dry sherry
sprigs of fresh mint, to garnish

Using a sharp knife, peel the papaya, cut it in half and scrape out the black pips. Cut the flesh into long slices and put into a small bowl. Peel the kiwi fruit, cut into slices and add to the bowl of papaya slices.

Skin the bananas and cut into slices. Put into another bowl and sprinkle with the lemon juice to stop them discolouring.

Now add the bananas to the other fruits and pour the sherry over them. Cover the bowl and leave to marinate for 2 hours in the refrigerator.

Spoon the fruits carefully into 4 glasses, adding a little of the sherry to each one. Garnish with mint and serve.

202 APRICOT FOOL

Preparation time:
10 minutes, plus soaking

Cooking time:
30 minutes

Serves 4

Calories:
218 per portion

YOU WILL NEED:
225 g/8 oz dried apricots, covered with
*   boiling water, soaked overnight, then*
*   simmered for 20-30 minutes until*
*   tender*
1 × 250 g/9 oz carton thick Greek
*   yogurt*
honey or fruit sugar, to taste
a few toasted flaked almonds

Purée the apricots in a food processor or blender. Mix with the yogurt. Sweeten to taste with honey or fruit sugar. Spoon into individual glasses or bowls; chill. Sprinkle with toasted almonds before serving.

■ COOK'S TIP

Papayas are large, greeny-yellow pear-shaped fruits that have an orange flesh. The dark seeds should be discarded. Buy when just beginning to soften.

■ COOK'S TIP

Instead of dried apricots, try using prunes, peaches or pears. Prunes will add a sweet taste, so will not need added sugar. Instead of almonds, try hazelnuts.

203 PEARS WITH FRESH RASPBERRY SAUCE

Preparation time:
about 20 minutes,
plus cooling

Cooking time:
10 minutes

Serves 4

Calories:
120 per portion

YOU WILL NEED:
4 large firm pears
300 ml/ ½ pint orange juice
bay leaf
small piece of cinnamon stick
1 tablespoon clear honey
225 g/8 oz fresh raspberries

Peel, halve and core the pears. Place them in a saucepan with the orange juice, bay leaf, cinnamon stick and honey. Cover the pan and simmer gently for 10 minutes.

Turn the pear halves over in their cooking liquid; cover the pan and leave them to cool in their liquid.

Blend the raspberries in a liquidizer until smooth; add sufficient of the pear cooking liquid to give a thin coating consistency.

Arrange the drained pear halves in a shallow serving dish and trickle over the prepared sauce.

204 GREENGAGE FOOL

Preparation time:
30 minutes, plus
chilling

Cooking time:
10-15 minutes

Serves 4

Calories:
85 per portion

YOU WILL NEED:
450 g/1 lb ripe fresh greengages
juice of 1 orange
150 ml/ ¼ pint skimmed milk
15 g/ ½ oz cornflour
sugar or artificial sweetener, to taste
4 tablespoons natural yogurt
halved orange slices, to garnish

Put the greengages into a pan with the orange juice; cover the pan and simmer gently until the fruit is just tender. Remove all the stones and cool.

Blend 2 tablespoons of the milk with the cornflour; heat the remaining milk in a pan and then stir into the cornflour paste. Return to the saucepan and stir over a gentle heat until the sauce has thickened. Add a little sugar or sweetener to taste.

Cool the sauce and then mix it with the cooled greengages; stir in the yogurt.

Spoon into stemmed glass dishes and chill for 2 hours before serving. Garnish each portion with a halved orange slice.

■ COOK'S TIP

Spoon the raspberry sauce on to individual serving plates; trickle a little natural yogurt on top, and arrange the pear halves carefully on top. Calories: per portion: 135.

■ COOK'S TIP

This is a low-fat fool, ideal for slimmers. Instead of the sauce, stir in 150 ml/ ¼ pint thick Greek yogurt or lightly whipped double cream for a richer dessert.

205 APPLE AND RAISIN PIE

Preparation time:
25 minutes, plus
chilling

Cooking time:
30 minutes

Oven temperature:
200 C/400 F/gas 6

Serves 6

Calories:
418 per portion

YOU WILL NEED:
300 g/10 oz wholemeal flour
150 g/5 oz margarine
4-5 tablespoons iced water
FOR THE FILLING
750 g/1 ½ lb dessert apples, peeled,
cored and thinly sliced
2 tablespoons light soft brown sugar
1 teaspoon ground cinnamon
4 cloves
50 g/2 oz raisins
1 teaspoon sesame seeds, to finish

Place the flour in a bowl and rub in the margarine until the
mixture resembles fine breadcrumbs. Stir in enough water to
mix to a dough. Turn on to a floured surface, knead lightly
until smooth, then divide in half. Roll out one piece thinly and
use to line a shallow 20 cm/8 inch pie dish.

Layer the apples with the sugar, spices and raisins in the
pastry case. Brush the pastry rim with water.

Roll out the remaining pastry and use to cover the pie. Seal
and pinch the edges well, then trim off any surplus pastry with
a sharp knife. Make a hole in the centre of the pie and chill for
20 minutes.

Brush with water and sprinkle with the sesame seeds. Bake
in a preheated moderately hot oven for 30-40 minutes, until
golden. Serve warm or cold with thick Greek yogurt or
whipped cream.

206 SLICED FIGS WITH LEMON SAUCE

Preparation time:
15-20 minutes

Serves 6

Calories:
110 per portion

YOU WILL NEED:
8 plump ripe figs
2 tablespoons lemon juice
150 ml/ ¼ pint unsweetened apple purée
(see Cook's Tip)
grated zest of ½ lemon
3 tablespoons natural yogurt
sugar or artificial sweetener, to taste
1 tablespoon chopped pistachio nuts
6 twists of lemon peel, to decorate
(optional)

Cut each fig into 4 wedges. (Alternatively, the figs can be sliced,
provided they are not too soft.) Sprinkle the cut figs with lemon
juice.

Mix the apple purée with the lemon zest and yogurt; add
sugar or artificial sweetener to taste and half the chopped
pistachios.

Spoon a pool of the lemon and pistachio sauce on to each of
6 small plates and arrange the pieces of fig decoratively on top.

Sprinkle with the remaining pistachio nuts and decorate
with twists of lemon peel, if liked.

■ COOK'S TIP

*The raisins in this dish will
plump up with the apple
juices. You could also add
some chopped dates and
reduce the amount of sugar
used.*

■ COOK'S TIP

*To make apple purée, peel
and core a large cooking
apple, such as a Bramley.
Immediately place in a
saucepan with a little water
and simmer until soft.*

207 PEAR AND GINGER PIE

Preparation time:
20 minutes

Cooking time:
30 minutes

Oven temperature:
200 C/400 F/gas 6

Serves 4-6

Calories:
480-320 per portion

YOU WILL NEED:
*225 g/8 oz plain flour or 100 per cent
  wholewheat flour*
100 g/4 oz butter or margarine
3 tablespoons cold water
FOR THE FILLING
1 teaspoon ground ginger
*750 g/1 ½ lb ripe dessert pears, peeled,
  cored and sliced*
2 tablespoons muscovado sugar
milk, to glaze

Sift the flour into a bowl, adding the bran left behind in the sieve. Rub in the fat with your fingertips until the mixture looks like breadcrumbs, then mix in the water to make a dough. Roll out half of the pastry on a floured board and use to line a 20-23 cm/8-9 inch pie plate. Sprinkle the ginger over the pastry, making sure that it is well distributed, then put the pears on top of the pastry and sprinkle with the sugar.

Roll out the rest of the pastry and use it to make a crust for the pie. Trim the pastry and crimp the edges of the pie with a fork. Make two or three holes for steam to escape and brush with milk.

Bake in a preheated oven for about 30 minutes, until the pastry is crisp and lightly browned. If the pears make a great deal of liquid, simply pour this off after you have cut the first slice of pie.

208 GINGER CREAMS

Preparation time:
15 minutes

Serves 6

Calories:
198 per portion

YOU WILL NEED:
*150 ml/ ¼ pint whipping cream, lightly
  whipped*
300 ml/ ½ pint natural yogurt
*75 g/3 oz ginger nut biscuits, finely
  crushed*
*25 g/1 oz crystallized or stem ginger,
  chopped*
*pieces of crystallized or stem ginger, to
  decorate*

Stir together the cream, yogurt and biscuits, then fold in the chopped ginger.

Spoon into individual glasses. Top each serving with pieces of ginger and serve with crisp biscuits.

■ COOK'S TIP

*This is a pleasant change
from the classic apple pie but
you could replace the pears
with the same quantity of
cooking apples, also peeled,
cored and sliced.*

■ COOK'S TIP

*To crush the ginger biscuits,
put them between sheets of
greaseproof paper and press
a rolling pin over them. Do
not reduce them to a
powder.*

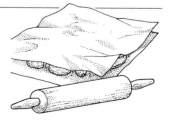

209 FRUIT AND NUT CRUMBLE

Preparation time:
15 minutes, plus
soaking

Cooking time:
45 minutes

Oven temperature:
200 C/400 F/gas 6

Serves 6

Calories:
452 per portion

YOU WILL NEED:

175 g/6 oz dried apricots
100 g/4 oz dried pitted prunes
100 g/4 oz dried figs
50 g/2 oz dried apples
600 ml/1 pint apple juice
175 g/6 oz wholemeal flour
75 g/3 oz margarine
50 g/2 oz dark soft brown sugar, sifted
50 g/2 oz hazelnuts, chopped

Place the dried fruits in a bowl with the apple juice and leave overnight. Transfer to a saucepan and simmer for 10-15 minutes, until softened. Turn into an ovenproof dish.

Place the flour in a bowl and rub in the margarine until the mixture resembles breadcrumbs. Stir in the sugar and hazelnuts, then sprinkle over the fruit.

Bake in a preheated oven for 25-30 minutes. Serve with some Greek yogurt.

210 ICED STUFFED APPLES

Preparation time:
35 minutes, plus
freezing

Cooking time:
5-6 minutes

Serves 4

Calories:
60 per portion

YOU WILL NEED:

2 medium cooking apples, peeled, cored
* and sliced*
4 tablespoons lemon juice
2 tablespoons brandy
2 egg yolks
3 tablespoons natural yogurt
4 red or green dessert apples
1 egg white
2 tablespoons sultanas

Stew the cooking apples with half the lemon juice in a covered pan until they are tender. Beat in the brandy and egg yolks and allow to cool.

Mix the yogurt with the cooked apple purée; pour into a shallow container and freeze until firm around the edges.

Cut a thin slice from the stalk end of each dessert apple, about 1 cm/½ inch thick and reserve for lids. Carefully hollow out the centre flesh and core, leaving a 'shell' about 5 mm/¼ inch thick. Brush inside with the remaining lemon juice.

Tip the semi-frozen apple mixture into a bowl and beat until smooth.

Whisk the egg white until stiff but not dry; fold lightly but thoroughly into the apple mixture, together with the sultanas.

Spoon the apple mixture into the hollow apples, and replace the lids. Open freeze until firm.

■ COOK'S TIP

As a topping variation use toasted chopped almonds instead of the hazelnuts, or stir in freshly grated coconut. Use soya margarine in the topping for a vegan version.

■ COOK'S TIP

Remove the frozen filled apples from the freezer a few minutes before serving to allow the centres to soften slightly. Sprinkle with a little cinnamon if desired.

211 YOGURT KNICKERBOCKER GLORY

Preparation time:
10 minutes

Serves 4

Calories:
290 per portion

YOU WILL NEED:
1 × 240 g/9 oz carton thick Greek yogurt
300 ml/ ½ pint raspberry yogurt, preferably with real fruit
2 large bananas, peeled and sliced
50 g/2 oz chopped hazelnuts

Layer the Greek yogurt, raspberry yogurt and banana attractively in four deep glasses, putting some of the banana slices down the sides of the glasses. Sprinkle the chopped nuts on top. Chill until ready to serve.

212 DATE AND APPLE SHORTCAKE

Preparation time:
25 minutes

Cooking time:
25 minutes

Oven temperature:
190 C/375 F/gas 5

Serves 8

Calories:
250 per portion

YOU WILL NEED:
FOR THE NUT PASTRY
75 g/3 oz margarine
40 g/1 ½ oz dark soft brown sugar
100 g/4 oz wholemeal flour
75 g/3 oz brazil nuts, ground
egg white
1 tablespoon chopped brazil nuts
FOR THE FILLING
3 tablespoons apple juice
450 g/1 lb dessert apples, peeled
100 g/4 oz dates, chopped
1 teaspoon ground cinnamon
150 ml/ ¼ pint double cream, whipped

Beat the margarine and sugar together until softened. Stir in the flour and ground nuts and mix to a firm dough. Turn on to a floured surface; knead lightly until smooth. Divide in half and roll each piece into a 20 cm/8 inch round on a baking sheet. Brush one with egg white and sprinkle with the nuts.

Bake in a preheated moderately hot oven for 10-15 minutes, until golden. Cut the nut-covered round into 8 sections while warm. Transfer both rounds to a wire rack to cool.

Place the apple juice in a pan and slice the apples into it. Cover and cook gently for about 10 minutes, stirring occasionally, until just soft. Add the dates and cinnamon. Cool.

Spread the apple filling over the whole shortcake round, cover with the cream and the cut top.

■ COOK'S TIP

Try using strawberry or mandarin yogurt instead of raspberry. Add some fresh fruit to complement the yogurt, if available.

■ COOK'S TIP

Instead of brazil nuts, use hazelnuts or almonds. Curd or cream cheese could be used instead of cream. Mix with a little milk and sugar until a creamy texture.

213 STRAWBERRY AND YOGURT ICE

Preparation time:
25 minutes, plus
freezing

Cooking time:
10 minutes

Serves 4

Calories:
363 per portion

YOU WILL NEED:
100 g/4 oz caster sugar
300 ml/ ½ pint water
350 g/12 oz fresh strawberries
300 ml/ ½ pint strawberry yogurt
1 egg white
150 ml/5 fl oz double cream

Put the sugar and water into a small pan and heat gently to dissolve the sugar, then boil rapidly until the thread stage is reached (see Cook's Tip). Leave to cool.

Reserve 4 strawberries for decoration, slice the rest and put into a blender or food processor with the syrup. Blend for a few seconds and pour into a bowl. Stir the yogurt into the strawberries and pour into a 1.2 litre/2 pint freezer container. Freeze for about 2 hours, stirring once or twice, until mushy, then spoon into a large mixing bowl.

Beat the egg white until stiff. Whisk the cream until it forms soft peaks, and beat the strawberry mixture until smooth. There is no need to wash your whisk if you keep to this order.

With a metal spoon fold the egg white and cream into the strawberry mixture until blended. Pour into the container and freeze for about 3 hours until the ice cream is setting round the edges. Spoon into a bowl and whisk until smooth and light. Pour back into the container, cover and freeze at least 6 hours. Serve decorated with the reserved strawberries.

214 MANGO SORBET WITH CARDAMOM SAUCE

Preparation time:
20 minutes, plus
freezing

Serves 4

Calories:
129 per portion

YOU WILL NEED:
2 large ripe mangoes, halved, peeled,
    stones removed and flesh cut into
    even-sized chunks
2 egg whites
FOR THE SAUCE
1 teaspoon cardamom pods
3 tablespoons clear honey
3 tablespoons orange juice
a few pistachio nuts, shelled and
    chopped, to decorate

Blend the mango flesh, which should make about 600 ml/1 pint of purée. Put this into a polythene container and freeze until firm round the edges.

Whisk the egg whites until stiff. Add the cold mango purée to the egg whites a little at a time, continuing to whisk. Put this mixture back into the freezer and freeze until firm. Meanwhile make the sauce. Crush the cardamom pods and remove the black seeds. Crush the seeds as finely as you can. Then mix with the honey and orange juice. Cover and leave for at least 30 minutes for the flavours to blend.

Just before serving, strain the sauce. Remove the sorbet from the freezer 30 minutes before it is required. Serve in individual bowls with the cardamom sauce and a few chopped pistachio nuts on top.

■ COOK'S TIP

When boiling sugar syrup the thread stage temperature is 107 C/225 F, on a sugar boiling thermometer. To test without a thermometer remove a little of the syrup with a small spoon and allow it to fall from the spoon on to a dish. The syrup should form a fine thread.

■ COOK'S TIP

The mango is a rich source of vitamins A and C. If the fruit is not ripe when purchased, keep it in a warm temperature for a few days to ripen before use.

215 MELON ICE CREAM

Preparation time:
20-25 minutes, plus freezing

Serves 4

Calories:
65 per portion

YOU WILL NEED:
1 medium melon (Ogen or Charentais)
300 ml/ ½ pint natural yogurt
artificial sweetener (optional)
small melon balls, to decorate

Halve the melon and scoop out all the seeds; scoop the melon flesh into a liquidizer, and blend until smooth.

Mix the melon purée with the yogurt and add artificial sweetener to taste. Transfer the melon and yogurt mixture to a shallow container, and freeze until firm.

Serve the melon ice cream in scoops, decorated with the small melon balls.

216 RASPBERRY AND PISTACHIO ICE CREAM

Preparation time:
20-25 minutes, plus freezing

Serves 4

Calories:
720 per portion

YOU WILL NEED:
350 g/12 oz fresh raspberries, washed
175 g/6 oz sugar or honey
450 ml/ ¾ pint whipping cream
100 g/4 oz pistachio nuts, chopped

Blend then sieve the raspberries to remove the pips and make a smooth purée. Add the sugar or honey. Whip the cream until it is thick, then fold in the raspberry purée. Pour the mixture into a plastic container and freeze until half-frozen, then stir well and add most of the pistachio nuts, reserving a few for decoration. Return to the freezer and freeze until solid.

Remove the ice cream from the freezer 30 minutes before serving. Spoon into individual bowls and sprinkle with the chopped pistachio nuts.

■ COOK'S TIP

For a richer, creamier dessert, use Greek yogurt or double cream instead of the natural yogurt. Try adding chopped crystallized ginger for a delicious spicy flavour.

■ COOK'S TIP

Any combination of fruit and nuts can be used for this recipe. Try blackcurrants with hazelnuts, or strawberries or apricots with almonds.

217 FIG CUSTARD TART

Preparation time:
20 minutes, plus
soaking

Cooking time:
35 minutes

Oven temperature:
200 C/400 F/gas 6
then
190 C/375 F/gas 5

Serves 4

Calories:
610 per portion

YOU WILL NEED:
75 g/3 oz plain wholewheat flour
75 g/3 oz plain white flour
pinch of salt
75 g/3 oz hard vegetable margarine
1 egg yolk
1 tablespoon water
1 tablespoon vegetable oil
FOR THE FILLING
175 g/6 oz dried figs, sliced
3 tablespoons clear honey
1 tablespoon lemon juice
150 ml/5 fl oz single cream
4 tablespoons milk
1 egg, beaten
1 tablespoon coarsely chopped walnuts

Put the flours and salt into a bowl and rub in the margarine. Make a well in the centre, add the egg yolk, water and oil. Mix to a dough. Roll out on a floured surface and line a 20 cm/8 inch fluted flan ring on a baking sheet. Bake for 15 minutes to set the pastry without browning. Remove and cool in the tin on a wire tray. Reduce the oven temperature.

For the filling, put the figs in a bowl with the honey and lemon juice, stir well, cover and leave to soak for about an hour to absorb most of the liquid.

Arrange the figs evenly over the cooked pastry case. Stir the cream and milk into the beaten egg. Pour over the figs and sprinkle the walnuts on the top. Bake for about 20 minutes, until the custard is just set and not browned. Cool in the tin.

■ COOK'S TIP

For this dish, use whole loose figs – the moist ready-to-eat variety that are widely available from supermarkets. You could use stoned prunes instead if preferred.

218 CHOCOLATE ROULADE

Preparation time:
30 minutes, plus
cooling

Cooking time:
15 minutes

Oven temperature:
200 C/400 F/gas 6

Serves 4

Calories:
827 per portion

YOU WILL NEED:
5 eggs, separated
175 g/6 oz soft brown sugar
3 tablespoons hot water
175 g/6 oz plain chocolate, melted
icing sugar
300 ml/½ pint whipping cream,
whipped

Grease a 25 × 35 cm/10 × 14 inch Swiss roll tin and line with a piece of greaseproof paper.

Put the egg yolks into a bowl with the sugar and whisk until thick and pale. Mix the hot water with the melted chocolate then gently stir this into the egg yolk mixture. Whisk the egg whites until stiff, then fold these gently into the mixture. Pour the mixture into the tin, quickly spreading it out to the edges.

Bake in a preheated oven for 15 minutes until well-risen and just firm to the touch. Cool the mixture in the tin for 10 minutes, then cover with a damp teacloth and leave for 10 minutes or overnight.

Remove the cloth, turn the cake out on to a piece of greaseproof paper that has been generously dusted with icing sugar. Carefully remove the greaseproof paper from the top of the cake, then leave to cool completely. When cold, trim the edges and spread with the whipped cream, then carefully roll the cake up, using the paper to help. Sprinkle with icing sugar.

■ COOK'S TIP

Decorate the roulade with chocolate curls, peeled from a block of plain chocolate, if liked. Fresh rosebuds on the plate would also look very pretty.

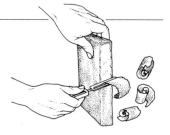

219 APPLE AND PEAR CRUMBLE

Preparation time:
15 minutes

Cooking time:
30 minutes

Oven temperature:
190 C/375 F/gas 5

Serves 4

Calories:
153 per portion

YOU WILL NEED:
225 g/8 oz apples, peeled, cored and sliced
225 g/8 oz pears, peeled, cored and sliced
grated zest of 1 lemon
½ teaspoon ground cinnamon
1 tablespoon water
1 tablespoon honey
FOR THE TOPPING
75 g/3 oz Swiss-style muesli
25 g/1 oz porridge oats

Place the apples and pears in a pan with the lemon zest, cinnamon, water and honey. Cook gently until the fruit is soft, but not pulpy. Spoon into a 1.2 litre/2 pint ovenproof dish.

Mix together the muesli and porridge oats and pile on top of the fruit. Cook in a preheated oven for 15 minutes or until the topping is crisp. Serve hot.

COOK'S TIP

Instead of the pears, try adding 225 g/8 oz cranberries, loganberries, tayberries or raspberries, adding more honey as required.

220 PLUM CHEESECAKE

Preparation time:
40 minutes, plus cooling and chilling

Cooking time:
1¼ hours

Oven temperature:
180 C/350 F/gas 4 then
160 C/325 F/gas 3

Serves 6-8

Calories:
333-250 per portion

YOU WILL NEED:
100 g/4 oz self-raising flour
25 g/1 oz light soft brown sugar
50 g/2 oz hard vegetable margarine
2 tablespoons vegetable oil
450 g/1 lb plums, halved and stoned
¼ teaspoon ground cinnamon
filling (see Cook's Tip)

Put the flour, sugar, margarine and oil into a bowl and knead to form a soft dough. Press the dough evenly over the base of a greased loose-bottomed 20 cm/8 inch cake tin. Bake near the top of a preheated oven for 20 minutes until golden brown. Cool in the tin. Reduce the oven temperature.

Arrange the plum halves close together over the base in the tin, cut-side down. Sprinkle with the cinnamon.

To complete the filling, fold the egg whites into the cheese mixture and spoon over the plums on the cheesecake base. Bake in the centre of the oven for 1¼ hours until the top is brown and firm then turn off the oven and slightly open the door. Leave the cheesecake to cool in the open oven for 1 hour.

Run a knife round the edge of the cheesecake to loosen it and gently ease it out of the tin. Slide the cheesecake on to a serving plate and chill in the refrigerator for up to 3 hours.

COOK'S TIP

For filling, whisk together 225 g/8 oz Quark or curd cheese, 50 g/2 oz brown sugar, vanilla essence, 150 ml/¼ pint soured cream, 1 tablespoon flour and 3 egg yolks. In another bowl whisk 3 egg whites until stiff then whisk in 50 g/2 oz brown sugar.

BAKING

Nobody can resist freshly baked and wholesome bread and cakes. Using wholemeal flour, dried fruits, nuts and oats, the recipes here are not only delicious but healthy too. Choose Malted wholemeal bread or Sage dairy bread to serve with one of the salads or soups in earlier chapters. Wheatgerm, honey and raisin muffins or Honey teacakes are good with fresh fruit desserts and the richer fruit cakes are delicious with afternoon tea.

221 MALTED WHOLEMEAL BREAD

Preparation time:
30 minutes, plus proving

Cooking time:
40 minutes

Oven temperature:
220 C/425 F/gas 7

Makes 4 500 g/1 lb loaves

Calories:
1,251 per loaf

Suitable for vegans

YOU WILL NEED:
1.5 kg/3 lb wholemeal flour
50 g/2 oz fine oatmeal
1 tablespoon salt
25 g/1 oz fresh yeast
900 ml-1.2 litres/1 ½-2 pints warm water
2 teaspoons malt extract
2 tablespoons oil
2 tablespoons rolled oats

Mix the flour, oatmeal and salt in a bowl. Mix the yeast with a little water and leave until frothy. Add to the flour with the remaining water, malt extract and oil and mix to a smooth dough. Turn on to a floured surface and knead for 8-10 minutes until smooth and elastic. Place in a clean bowl, cover with a damp cloth and leave to rise for 2 hours.

Turn on to a floured surface, knead for a few minutes, then divide into 4. Shape and place in greased 450 g/1 lb loaf tins. Brush with water and sprinkle with the oats. Cover and leave to rise in a warm place for about 30 minutes, until the dough just reaches the top of the tins. Bake in a preheated hot oven for 15 minutes. Lower the temperature to 190 C/375 F/gas 5, and bake for a further 20-25 minutes.

▨ COOK'S TIP

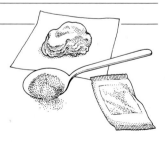

Fresh yeast is generally available from health food shops. If not, use easy blend yeast from supermarkets which can be added directly to the dry ingredients.

222 RYE BREAD

Preparation time:
20 minutes, plus proving

Cooking time:
55 minutes

Oven temperature:
220 C/425 F/gas 7

Makes 2 loaves

Calories:
755 per loaf

Suitable for vegans

YOU WILL NEED:
350 g/12 oz rye flour
450 g/1 lb wholemeal flour
2 teaspoons salt
25 g/1 oz fresh yeast
450-600 ml/¾-1 pint warm water
2 tablespoons black treacle
2 tablespoons oil
milk for brushing
1 teaspoon caraway seeds

Mix the flours and salt together in a bowl. Cream the yeast with a little of the water and leave until frothy. Add to the flour mixture with the remaining water, treacle and oil and mix thoroughly to a firm dough. Turn on to a floured surface and knead for 5 minutes until smooth and elastic. Place in a clean bowl, cover with a damp cloth and leave to rise in a warm place for 2 hours, until doubled in size.

Turn on to a floured surface and knead for a few minutes. Shape into 2 oval loaves and place on greased baking sheets. Prick with a fork. Leave to rise for 1 ½ hours, until doubled in size. Brush with milk and sprinkle with caraway seeds. Bake in a preheated hot oven for 15 minutes. Lower the heat to 190 C/375 F/gas 5, and bake for a further 30-40 minutes. Cool on a wire rack.

▨ COOK'S TIP

Caraway seeds add an unusual light aniseed flavour to this bread. Instead, try fennel or cumin seeds, the former being similar to caraway and the latter having a distinct flavour of their own.

223 SAGE DAIRY BREAD

Preparation time:
15 minutes

Cooking time:
25 minutes

Oven temperature:
220 C/425 F/gas 7

Makes 1 loaf

Calories:
160 per average slice

YOU WILL NEED:
225 g/8 oz wholewheat flour
225 g/8 oz granary flour, plus extra for
    sprinkling
1 teaspoon salt
2 teaspoons baking powder
1 teaspoon bicarbonate of soda
100 g/4 oz low-fat vegetarian cottage
    cheese
1 tablespoon chopped fresh sage, or
    1 teaspoon dried sage
1 teaspoon lemon juice
about 50-85 ml/2-3 fl oz skimmed milk,
    plus extra for brushing

Sift the flours, salt, baking powder and soda into a mixing bowl and tip in the bran remaining in the sieve. Stir in the cottage cheese and sage and sprinkle on the lemon juice. Pour on the milk, mixing all the time, adding just enough to make a soft dough. Knead the dough lightly until it is smooth and free from cracks.

Divide the dough into 4 pieces. Shape each one into a ball. Place the rounds close together on a greased and floured baking sheet to form a 'crown'. Brush the tops lightly with milk and sprinkle lightly with granary flour.

Bake the bread in a preheated oven for about 25 minutes or until it is well risen and firm and sounds hollow when tapped underneath. Cool the bread on a wire tray.

224 DATE AND CINNAMON SCONES

Preparation time:
20 minutes

Cooking time:
15 minutes

Oven temperature:
220 C/425 F/gas 7

Makes 10-12

Calories:
101-84 per portion

YOU WILL NEED:
225 g/8 oz plain wholewheat flour
4 teaspoons baking powder
2 teaspoons cinnamon
pinch of salt
50 g/2 oz butter or margarine
50 g/2 oz muscovado sugar
75 g/3 oz dates, chopped
175 ml/6 fl oz milk and water mixed
extra flour for rolling out

Sift the flour, baking powder and cinnamon and salt into a bowl, adding any bran left in the sieve. Rub in the fat, then add the sugar, dates and milk. Mix to a dough, then turn it out on to a floured board and knead gently for a minute or two; the consistency will be sticky and soft.

Place the dough on a lightly floured board and roll or pat out to a thickness of 2 cm/¾ inch. Cut out the scones using a 5 cm/2 inch round cutter. Put the scones on a baking tray and bake in a preheated oven for 10-15 minutes, until risen and firm. Cool on a wire rack. Serve warm.

■ COOK'S TIP

Instead of sage, try adding fresh rosemary or thyme – they are both delicious and aromatic. Eat this loaf warm and on the day of baking, as it is then at its best.

■ COOK'S TIP

Vary the scones by using other spices, fruits and nuts. Try raisin and ginger scones, replacing the cinnamon with ground ginger and the dates with raisins.

225 WALNUT SODA BREAD

Preparation time:
15 minutes

Cooking time:
40 minutes

Oven temperature:
190 C/375 F/gas 5

**Makes one 18 cm/
7 inch round loaf**

Calories:
215 per average slice

YOU WILL NEED:
450 g/1 lb wholewheat flour
2 teaspoons baking powder
1 teaspoon salt
1 tablespoon light muscovado sugar
75 g/3 oz chopped walnuts
300 ml/½ pint natural yogurt
water to mix
2 tablespoons milk
2 tablespoons cracked wheat

Sift the flour, baking powder and salt into a mixing bowl and stir in the sugar and walnuts. Stir in the yogurt and sufficient water to make a firm dough.

Knead the dough lightly in the bowl until it is smooth and free from cracks. Shape the dough into a round about 18 cm/7 inches in diameter and place it on a greased baking sheet. Mark the top into 4 segments. Brush the top with milk and sprinkle with the cracked wheat.

Bake the loaf in a preheated oven for 40 minutes, or until it is well risen and firm and sounds hollow when tapped underneath. Cool on a wire rack.

226 APRICOT AND GINGER SCONE BARS

Preparation time:
15 minutes

Cooking time:
25 minutes

Oven temperature:
220 C/425 F/gas 7

Makes 8 slices

Calories:
195 per slice

YOU WILL NEED:
225 g/8 oz wholewheat flour
1 teaspoon bicarbonate of soda
1 ½ teaspoons ground ginger
pinch of mixed ground spice
salt
75 g/3 oz soft margarine
100 g/4 oz dried apricot pieces, chopped
150 ml/¼ pint natural yogurt
2 tablespoons milk, for brushing
2 tablespoons demerara sugar

Sift the flour, soda, 1 teaspoon of the ginger, the mixed spice and salt into a mixing bowl and tip in the bran remaining in the sieve. Using a fork beat in the soft margarine and stir in the apricots. Stir in the yogurt and mix to form a ball. Knead the dough lightly until it is smooth.

Press the dough into a greased 18 cm/7 inch square baking tin. Brush the top with milk, sprinkle on the sugar mixed with the remaining ginger and mark the top into bars.

Bake the scone in a preheated oven for 25 minutes, until it is well risen and firm. Cool slightly in the tin, then transfer it to a wire rack. Cut into bars and serve warm.

■ COOK'S TIP

As nuts are high in fat, they tend to go rancid quickly. Store in airtight jars either in a cool, dry cupboard or the fridge. Nuts are also best freshly cracked.

■ COOK'S TIP

These are also delicious served cold. They are ideal for picnics or packed lunches. Add some chopped, blanched almonds for extra protein and flavour.

227 FIGGY SCONE BREAD

Preparation time:
20 minutes

Cooking time:
25 minutes

Oven temperature:
200 C/400 F/gas 6

**Makes one 20 cm/
8 inch round scone**

Calories:
200 per piece

YOU WILL NEED:
175 g/6 oz wholewheat flour
1 teaspoon baking powder
salt
25 g/1 oz light muscovado sugar
50 g/2 oz fine oatmeal
75 g/3 oz soft margarine
100 g/4 oz dried figs, finely chopped
about 150 ml/¼ pint skimmed milk
2 tablespoons clear honey, melted

Sift the flour, baking powder and salt into a mixing bowl, tip in any bran remaining in the sieve and stir in the sugar and oatmeal. Using a fork, beat in the margarine and stir in the figs and just enough milk to form a soft dough. Knead the dough lightly until it is smooth.

Press the dough into a greased 20 cm/8 inch round tin and mark into 6 wedges. Brush the top with honey.

Bake in a preheated oven for 25 minutes, or until the scone is well risen and golden brown. Cool the scone partly in the tin, then turn out on to a wire rack.

228 WHEATGERM, HONEY AND RAISIN MUFFINS

Preparation time:
15 minutes

Cooking time:
20 minutes

Oven temperature:
180 C/350 F/gas 4

Makes 12

Calories:
108 per portion

YOU WILL NEED:
100 g/4 oz wheatgerm
2 teaspoons baking powder
pinch of salt
75 g/3 oz raisins
4 tablespoons clear honey
50 g/2 oz butter or margarine, melted
2 small eggs
about 6 tablespoons milk

Grease a bun or muffin tin with butter. Put the wheatgerm, baking powder, salt and raisins into a bowl, then add the honey, butter or margarine and eggs. Mix until blended, then stir in enough milk to make a fairly soft mixture which drops heavily from the spoon when you shake it.

Put heaped tablespoons of the mixture into the bun tin, dividing the mixture between twelve sections. Bake in a pre-heated oven for 15-20 minutes, until the muffins have puffed up and feel firm to a light touch. Serve warm.

■ COOK'S TIP

This bread is good served warm. Spread it with cottage cheese for a calcium-rich snack. Add 50 g/2 oz chopped walnuts to the dough for extra protein.

■ COOK'S TIP

These muffins contain the goodness of wheatgerm and raisins and are quick and easy to make. Serve them warm from the oven with a fresh fruit salad.

229 HONEY TEACAKES

Preparation time:
30 minutes, plus
standing and rising

Cooking time:
25 minutes

Oven temperature:
220 C/425 F/gas 7

Makes 8

Calories:
300 per portion

YOU WILL NEED:
100 g/4 oz wholewheat flour
1 teaspoon light muscovado sugar
1 tablespoon dried yeast
175 ml/6 fl oz tepid skimmed milk
FOR THE DOUGH
350 g/12 oz wholewheat flour
salt
50 g/2 oz soft margarine
3 tablespoons clear honey, melted
75 g/3 oz chopped hazelnuts
1 egg, beaten
glaze (see Cook's Tip)

Mix together the flour, sugar and dried yeast, pour on the milk and mix to a smooth batter. Set aside in a warm place for about 15 minutes until the mixture is frothy.

For the dough, sift the flour and salt, rub in the margarine, and stir in the honey, nuts and egg. Pour on the yeast batter mixture and mix until the dough leaves the sides of the bowl. Turn out the dough on to a lightly floured board and knead for about 10 minutes, or until it is smooth and pliable. Shape the dough into a ball, return it to the bowl and cover with a piece of oiled polythene. Leave it in a warm place for about 45 minutes, or until it has doubled in size.

Knead the dough and divide it into 8 pieces. Shape into rounds and place them well apart on 2 baking sheets.

Bake the teacakes in a preheated oven for 20 minutes, or until they sound hollow when tapped underneath. Brush with the glaze and return to the oven for 2-3 minutes.

■ COOK'S TIP

For an easy, tasty glaze for the teacakes, mix together 1 tablespoon each light muscovado sugar and skimmed milk.

230 CARROT CAKE

Preparation time:
25 minutes, plus
cooling

Cooking time:
1 hour 10 minutes

Oven temperature:
180 C/350 F/gas 4

**Makes one 18 cm/
7 inch round cake**

Total Calories:
3,094

YOU WILL NEED:
225 g/8 oz light soft brown sugar
175 ml/6 fl oz vegetable oil
2 eggs
100 g/4 oz plain wholemeal flour
1 teaspoon ground cinnamon
1 teaspoon bicarbonate of soda
150 g/5 oz coarsely grated carrots
50 g/2 oz chopped walnuts
jam topping (see Cook's Tip)

Line an 18 cm/7 inch round cake tin with non-stick silicone paper or greaseproof paper. Use a fixed-base tin as the mixture is almost a pouring consistency.

Put the sugar into a mixing bowl and using an electric whisk gradually whisk the oil, then whisk in the eggs one at a time. Mix together the flour, cinnamon and bicarbonate of soda and stir into the egg mixture, then add the carrots and walnuts. Beat all the ingredients together with a wooden spoon then pour into the prepared tin.

Place in the centre of a preheated oven and bake for about 1 hour 10 minutes until the cake is risen and firm to the touch. Take from the oven, let stand in the tin for 3 minutes, then turn out on to a wire tray, peel off the paper and leave to cool.

Brush the topping generously over the top of the cooled cake and immediately sprinkle over the walnuts. The glaze will set very quickly.

■ COOK'S TIP

For the jam topping: boil together for 2-3 minutes 2 tablespoons apricot jam and 1 tablespoon lemon juice. Prepare 50 g/2 oz chopped walnuts.

231 ORANGE MARMALADE RING

Preparation time:
20 minutes

Cooking time:
1 hour 5 minutes

Oven temperature:
160 C/325 F/gas 3

**Makes one 23 cm/
9 inch cake ring**

Calories:
310 per piece (of 10)

YOU WILL NEED:
225 g/8 oz wholewheat flour
salt
2 teaspoons baking powder
1 teaspoon ground cinnamon
50 g/2 oz light muscovado sugar
*8 tablespoons low-sugar orange
    marmalade, chopped*
grated zest and juice of 1 orange
175 ml/6 fl oz vegetable oil
2 eggs
150 g/5 oz seedless raisins
2 tablespoons honey, melted, to glaze
orange zest strands, to decorate

Sift the flour, salt, baking powder and cinnamon into a bowl and tip in any bran remaining in the sieve. In another bowl mix together the sugar, marmalade, orange zest, orange juice and oil and beat in the eggs. Gradually beat in the flour mixture, and stir in the raisins.

Turn the mixture into a greased and floured 23 cm/9 inch metal ring mould. Bake in a preheated oven for 1 hour and 5 minutes, or until the cake is well risen and firm.

Leave the cake to cool a little in the ring, then turn it out on to a wire tray. Brush it with the melted honey while it is still warm. Cool the cake completely, then wrap it in foil.

232 FRUIT AND NUT CAKE

Preparation time:
20 minutes, plus
chilling

Cooking time:
5 minutes

**Makes 1 × 1 kg/2 lb
cake**

Total Calories:
3,915

YOU WILL NEED:
*225 g/8 oz digestive biscuits, coarsely
    crumbled*
175 g/6 oz candied peel, chopped
175 g/6 oz glacé cherries, chopped
100 g/4 oz raisins
100 g/4 oz shelled Brazil nuts, chopped
1 teaspoon ground mixed spice
3 tablespoons sherry
3 tablespoons black treacle
*100 g/4 oz plain chocolate, broken into
    pieces*
FOR THE DECORATION
shelled Brazil nuts
glacé cherries, halved

Lightly grease a 1 kg/2 lb loaf tin and line with greased grease-proof paper.

Mix the crumbled biscuits with the peel, cherries, raisins, nuts and mixed spice.

Place the sherry, black treacle and chocolate in a bowl. Stand the bowl over a saucepan of gently simmering water and stir until all the ingredients have melted. Stir the melted ingredients into the biscuit and fruit mixture, and mix thoroughly together.

Pour into the prepared loaf tin and spread the surface level. Cover with a piece of greased greaseproof paper. Chill until the cake is quite firm. Turn out and decorate with Brazil nuts and glacé cherries. Slice to serve.

■ COOK'S TIP

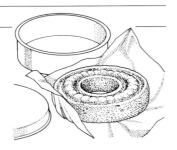

For a really moist cake, leave to mature for a few days, wrapped in foil and stored in an airtight container. It will keep well in this way for up to one week.

■ COOK'S TIP

The usual red glacé cherries, being dyed with cochineal, are not strictly vegetarian. Choose natural glacé cherries instead. Health food shops and supermarkets sell them.

233 VEGETARIAN MINCE PIES

Preparation time:
30 minutes

Cooking time:
10 minutes

Oven temperature:
200 C/400 F/gas 6

Makes 24

Calories:
130 per portion

YOU WILL NEED:
100 g/4 oz each currants, raisins and
sultanas
50 g/2 oz cooking dates, chopped
50 g/2 oz candied peel
50 g/2 oz glacé cherries, chopped
50 g/2 oz flaked almonds
1 ripe banana, chopped
4 tablespoons brandy or whisky
½ teaspoon each ground ginger, grated
nutmeg, mixed spice
FOR THE PASTRY
450 g/1 lb wholewheat flour
225 g/8 oz butter or margarine
10-12 teaspoons cold water

To make the mincemeat, simply mix everything together.

Lightly grease a shallow bun or muffin tin. Sift the flour and salt into a bowl, tipping in any bran left in the sieve, add the butter or margarine, and rub into the flour with your fingertips until the mixture resembles breadcrumbs. Add the water, then press the mixture together to make a dough.

Roll out the dough on a lightly-floured board, then cut out 12 cm/4¾ inch circles and 10 cm/4 inch circles using round cutters. Press one of the larger circles gently into each section of the bun or muffin tin, then put a heaped teaspoon of mincemeat into each and cover with the smaller pastry circles. Press down firmly at the edges, make a hole in the top for steam to escape, then bake for about 10 minutes, until the pastry is lightly browned. Cool in the tin.

■ COOK'S TIP

This mincemeat can be stored for a week in a covered bowl in the refrigerator, but doesn't keep in the same way as ordinary mincemeat because of the *lack of sugar. There is enough mincemeat here to fill about 36 pies in all.*

234 CHRISTMAS CARROT CAKE

Preparation time:
30 minutes, plus
soaking

Cooking time:
1¼ hours

Oven temperature:
180 C/350 F/gas 4

Serves 16

Calories:
300 per slice

YOU WILL NEED:
175 g/6 oz sultanas
4 tablespoons whisky
250 ml/8 fl oz corn oil
100 g/4 oz molasses sugar
3 eggs (size 1)
1 tablespoon cocoa powder
225 g/8 oz plain wholemeal flour
1 teaspoon cinnamon
½ teaspoon grated nutmeg
½ teaspoon allspice
½ teaspoon salt
1½ teaspoons baking powder
1½ teaspoons bicarbonate of soda
225 g/8 oz carrots, finely grated
75 g/3 oz walnuts, finely chopped
icing (see Cook's Tip)

Soak the sultanas in the whisky for 1 hour or more. Line a loose bottomed 20 cm/8 inch cake tin with non-stick silicone, or greased and floured greaseproof paper.

Beat together the oil and sugar, adding the eggs one at a time. (At this stage the mixture looks very odd, but don't worry.) Still beating, add the cocoa powder, flour, spices, salt, baking powder and bicarbonate of soda.

Mix in the carrots, the sultanas and the whisky, and the nuts. Tip the mixture into the cake tin. Bake in a preheated oven for about 1¼ hours; a warmed skewer will come out clean when the cake is cooked. Allow the cake to cool in the tin. When it is quite cold, spread over the icing.

■ COOK'S TIP

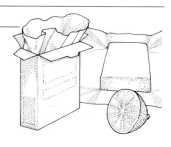

For the icing, work 50 g/2 oz icing sugar into 350 g/12 oz low-fat soft cheese. Add the finely grated zest of ½ a lemon. Spread the icing over the top of the cake.

235 CHOCOLATE BISCUIT SQUARES

Preparation time:
15-20 minutes, plus chilling

Makes 9

Calories:
329 per biscuit

YOU WILL NEED:
175 g/6 oz plain chocolate
50 g/2 oz butter or margarine
225 g/8 oz digestive biscuits
grated zest of 1 orange
100 g/4 oz sultanas
50 g/2 oz natural glacé cherries, chopped
icing sugar, sifted, to decorate

Melt the chocolate and butter in a heatproof bowl over a pan of hot water. Remove from the heat.

Put the biscuits in a polythene bag and crush with a rolling pin. Add to the chocolate mixture with the orange zest, sultanas and chopped cherries. Mix well and press into an 18 cm/ 7 inch square tin. Mark into 9 squares.

Chill well before cutting into squares. Sprinkle with a little icing sugar before serving.

236 MARZIPAN AND APPLE PIES

Preparation time:
35 minutes, plus chilling

Cooking time:
20 minutes

Oven temperature:
220 C/425 F/gas 7

Makes 20 pies

Calories:
184 per portion

YOU WILL NEED:
350 g/12 oz wholemeal self-raising flour
pinch of salt
225 g/8 oz hard vegetable margarine, from the freezer
scant 7 tablespoons water
2 tablespoons vegetable oil
275 g/10 oz Bramley apples, peeled, cored and coarsely chopped
100 g/4 oz bought marzipan, cut into 5 mm/¼ inch cubes
milk, for brushing

Make the pastry. Put the flour and salt into a bowl. Grate the margarine straight into the flour, dipping the grater into the bowl now and again to free the flakes of margarine. Distribute the margarine gently through the flour, using a round-bladed knife, then add the water and oil. Mix to a fairly firm dough then put into a polythene bag and chill for 1 hour if possible.

Mix the apples and marzipan together in a bowl. Roll out the pastry quite thinly on a lightly floured surface. Cut out 40 rounds using a 7½ cm/3 inch fluted cutter.

Line 20 small tartlet tins with half the rounds, and spoon the filling into them, packing it in well. Brush both sides of the remaining rounds with milk and lay them on top of the tartlets in the tin. Press the edges together to seal.

Bake near the top of the preheated oven for 15-20 minutes until golden brown. Lift carefully from the tin and leave to cool slightly on a wire tray. Serve warm or cold.

■ COOK'S TIP

If preferred, omit the glacé cherries and increase the quantity of sultanas in these biscuits.

■ COOK'S TIP

These tempting little pies make the perfect vegetarian alternative to traditional mince pies. Sprinkle them with a little demerara sugar before baking, if liked.

237 MUESLI SQUARES

Preparation time:
10 minutes

Cooking time:
20 minutes

Oven temperature:
180 C/350 F/gas 4

Makes 18

Calories:
120 per biscuit

YOU WILL NEED:
3 tablespoons honey
100 g/4 oz butter
50 g/2 oz soft light brown sugar
50 g/2 oz chopped mixed nuts
100 g/4 oz porridge oats
25 g/1 oz desiccated coconut
50 g/2 oz sesame seeds

Place the honey, butter and sugar in a saucepan. Heat gently until the butter has melted and the sugar has dissolved. Stir in the nuts, oats, coconut and sesame seeds.

Press evenly into a greased 28 × 18 cm (11 × 7 inch) shallow oblong tin. Bake in a preheated oven for 20 minutes, until golden brown.

Cool for 5 minutes in the tin, then cut into squares. Leave in the tin to cool completely.

238 CRISPY CRACKLES

Preparation time:
10 minutes, plus cooling

Cooking time:
3 minutes

Makes 16

Calories:
57 per biscuit

YOU WILL NEED:
50 g/2 oz butter or margarine
2 tablespoons golden syrup
50 g/2 oz drinking chocolate powder, sifted
50 g/2 oz cornflakes

Melt the butter and golden syrup over a low heat. Remove from the heat and stir in the drinking chocolate and cornflakes, mixing well so that the cornflakes are well coated in the chocolate syrup mixture.

Spoon into paper cases, set on a baking sheet, and leave to cool. They will set on cooling.

■ COOK'S TIP

For a delicious variation, melt 100 g/4 oz plain chocolate and dip one side of each cold square in it. Sit the squares on a wire rack to let the chocolate harden.

■ COOK'S TIP

Use plain cornflakes for this recipe, not ones with added chopped nuts, honey or sugar. Or try a different cereal such as Rice Crispies or bran flakes.

239 AMERICAN BRAN MUFFINS

Preparation time:
10 minutes

Cooking time:
15 minutes

Oven temperature:
200 C/400 F/gas 6

Makes 24

Calories:
106 per muffin

YOU WILL NEED:
4 tablespoons oil
75 g/3 oz soft dark brown sugar
75 g/3 oz golden syrup
2 eggs, beaten
250 ml/8 fl oz milk
50 g/2 oz bran
75 g/3 oz raisins
100 g/4 oz self-raising flour
1 teaspoon baking powder
½ teaspoon bicarbonate of soda
½ teaspoon salt

Place the oil, sugar, syrup, beaten eggs and milk in a large bowl. Mix thoroughly with a fork.

Add the bran and raisins and sift in the flour, baking powder, bicarbonate of soda and salt. Stir very lightly until the ingredients are just mixed.

Spoon the mixture into paper cake cases or greased bun tins until a scant two-thirds full.

Bake in a preheated oven for 15 minutes, until well risen and firm to the touch. Serve warm, split in half and buttered.

240 TREACLE & SULTANA FLAPJACKS

Preparation time:
10 minutes

Cooking time:
40 minutes

Oven temperature:
160 C/325 F/gas 3

Makes 12

Calories:
213 per biscuit

YOU WILL NEED:
150 g/5 oz butter
75 g/3 oz Barbados or molasses sugar
1-2 tablespoons black molasses
50 g/2 oz sultanas
225 g/8 oz jumbo or rolled oats
grated zest and juice of ½ lemon

Melt the butter in a saucepan. Stir in the sugar and molasses. Add the sultanas, oats and lemon zest and juice and mix well. Press into a greased 25 × 20 cm/10 × 8 inch tin.

Bake in a preheated oven for 40 minutes. Allow to cool for 10 minutes, then cut into bars. Leave the flapjacks in the tin until completely cold.

■ COOK'S TIP

Unlike traditional British muffins, American muffins are deep and have a cake-like texture. Bake them in bun tins or in individual paper cases.

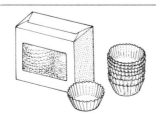

■ COOK'S TIP

Try currants instead of sultanas in these flapjacks. If molasses is unavailable, use black treacle or golden syrup instead.

INDEX